Sea Horse Adult Coloring Book

This Coloring book belongs to:

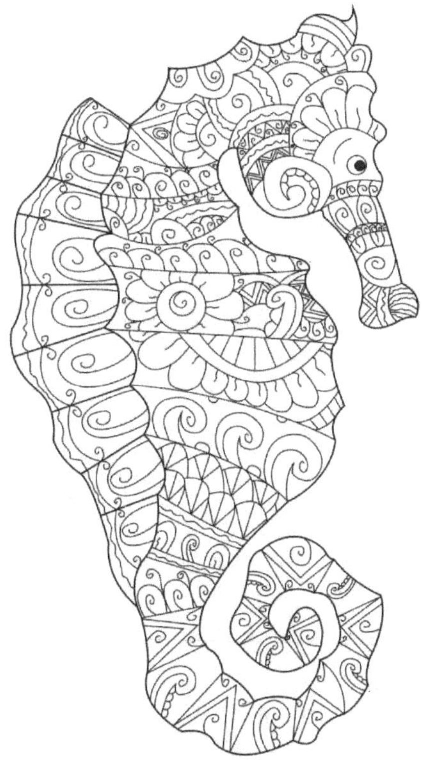

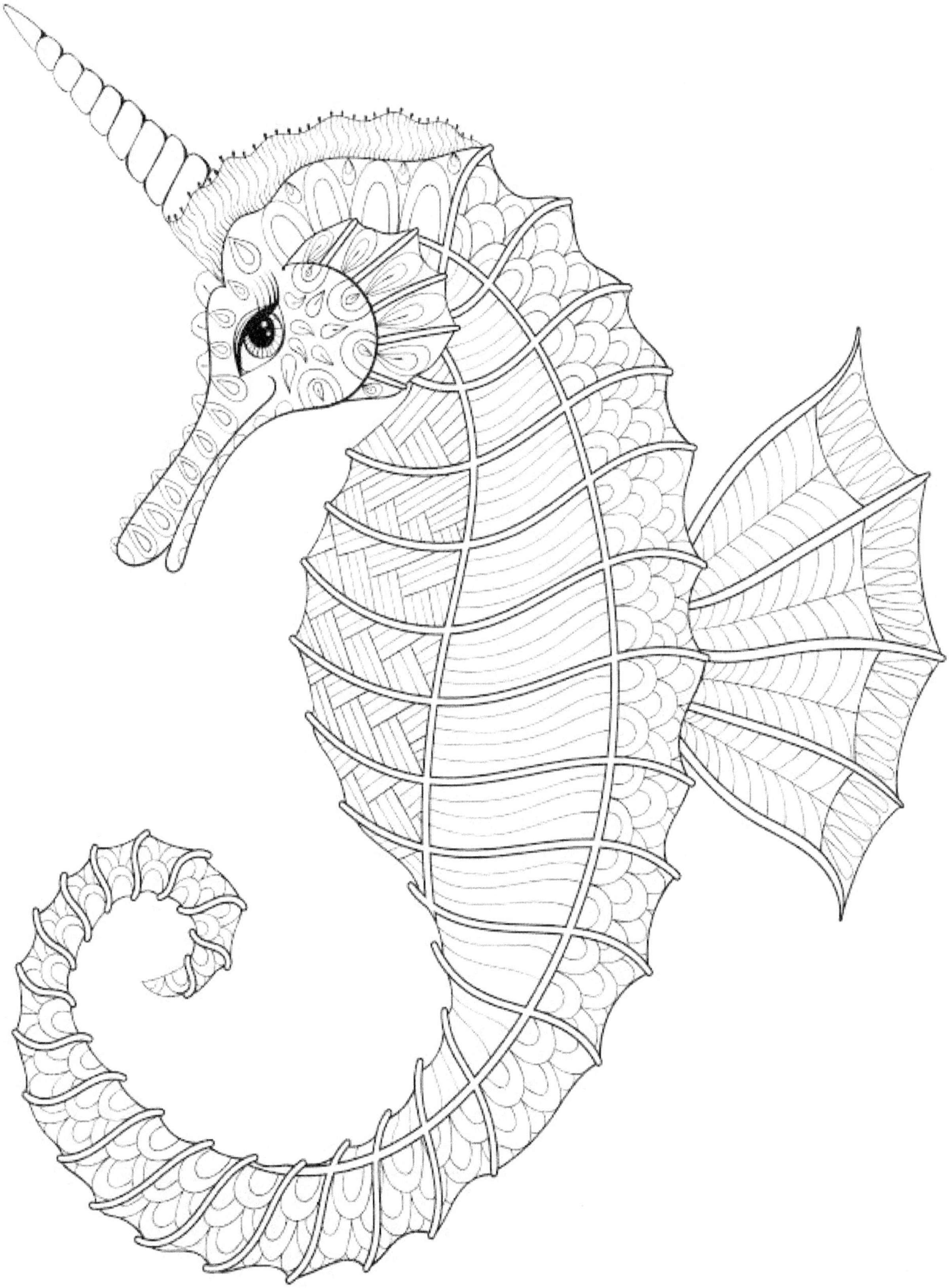

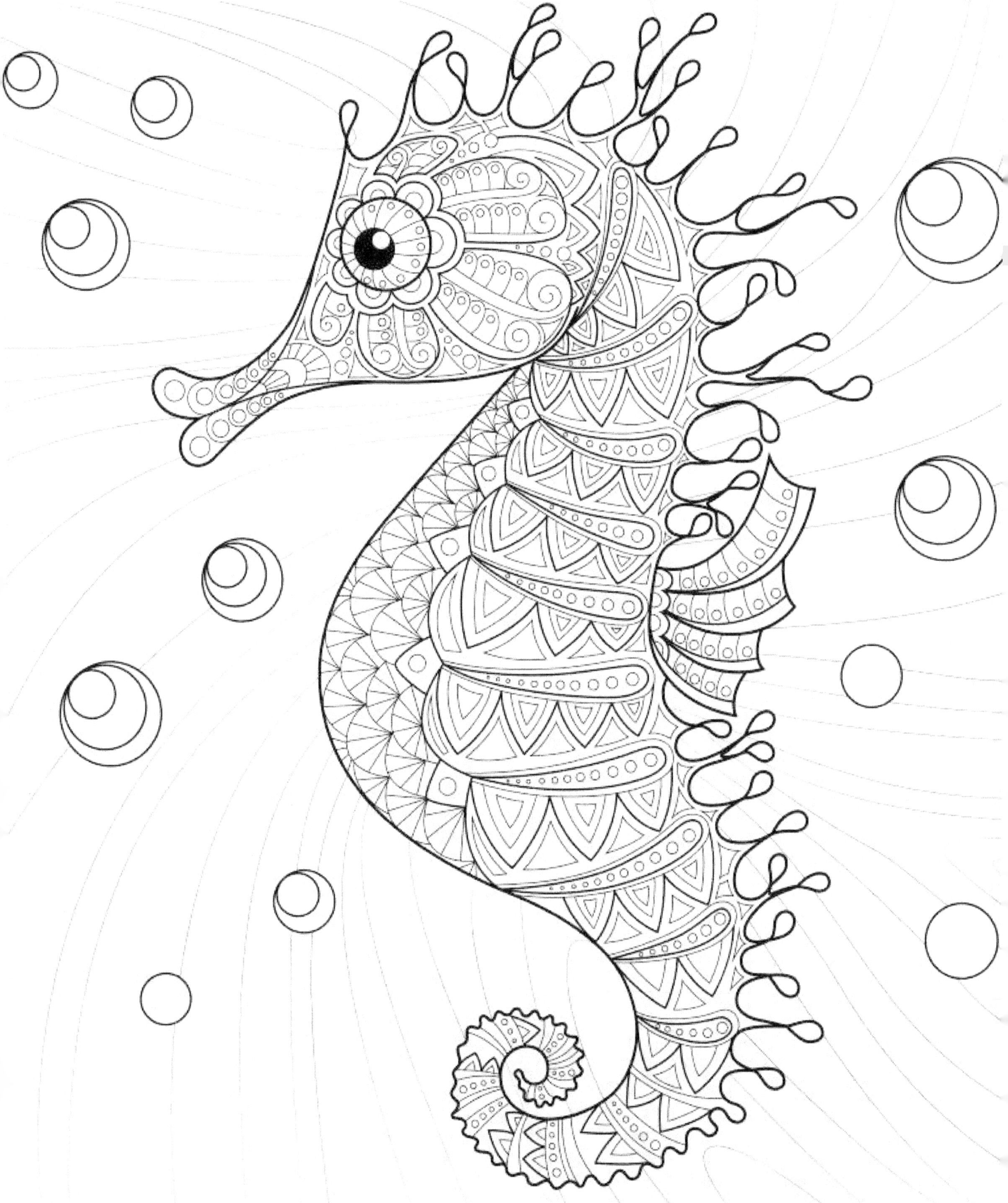

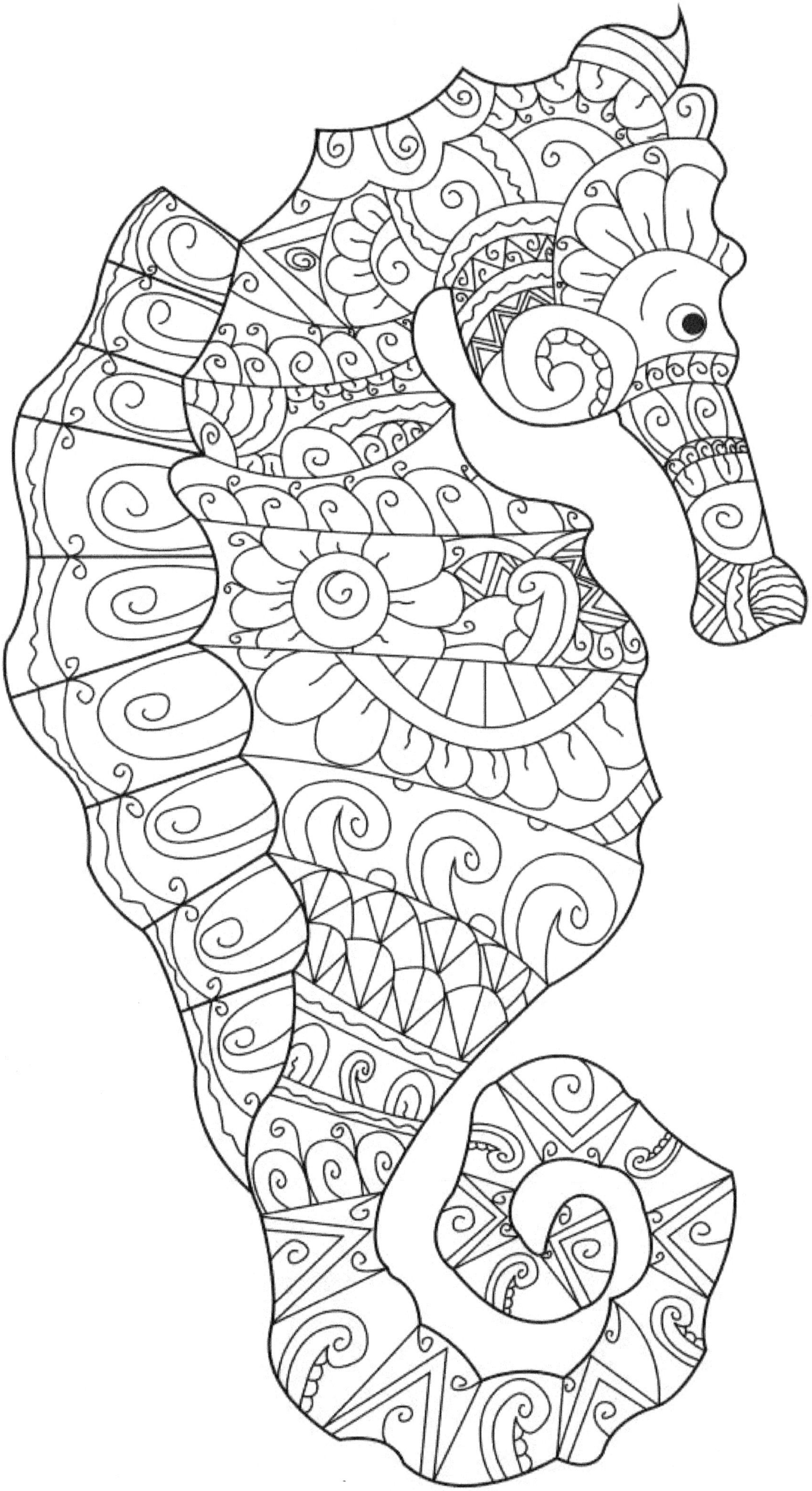

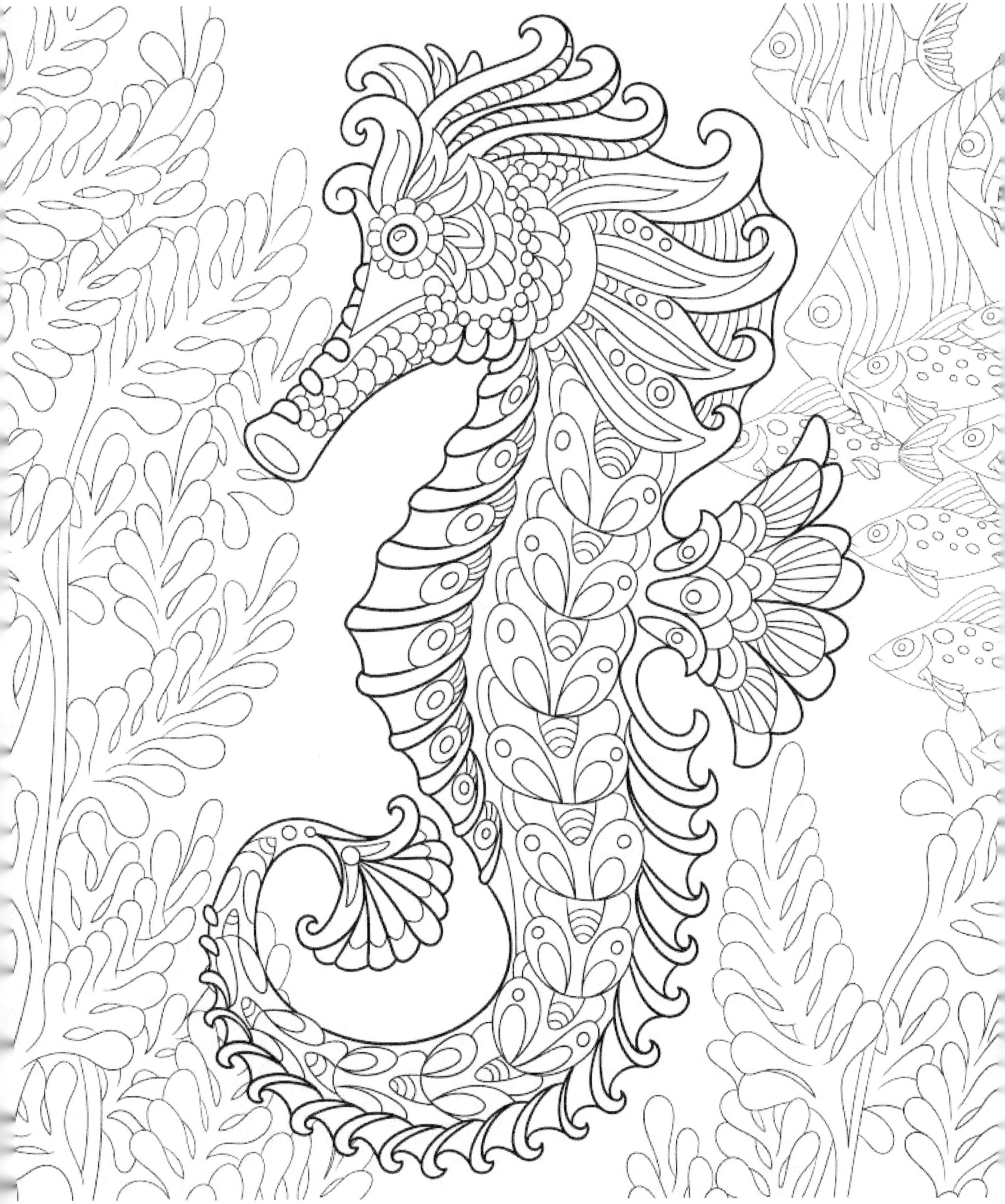

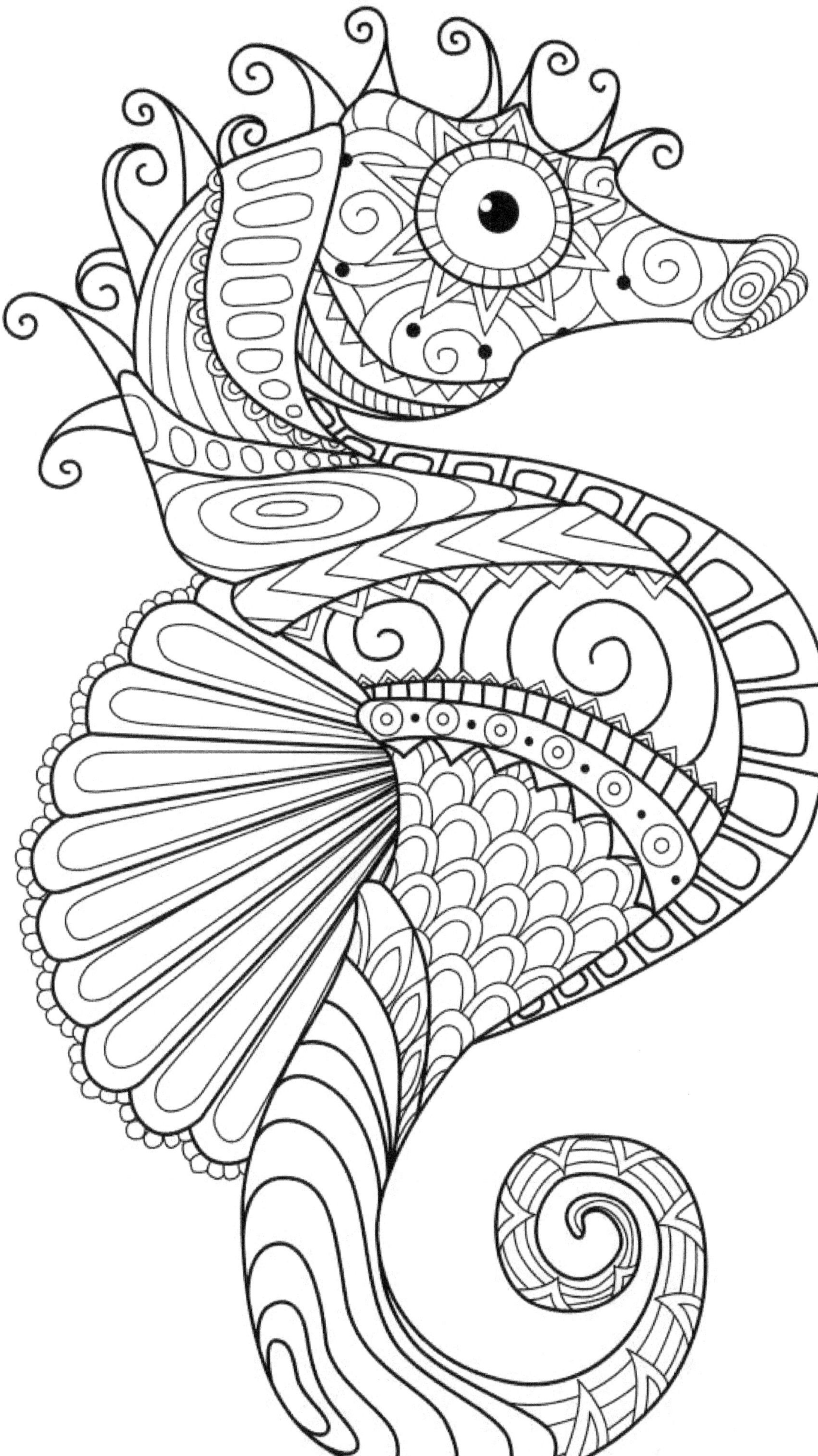

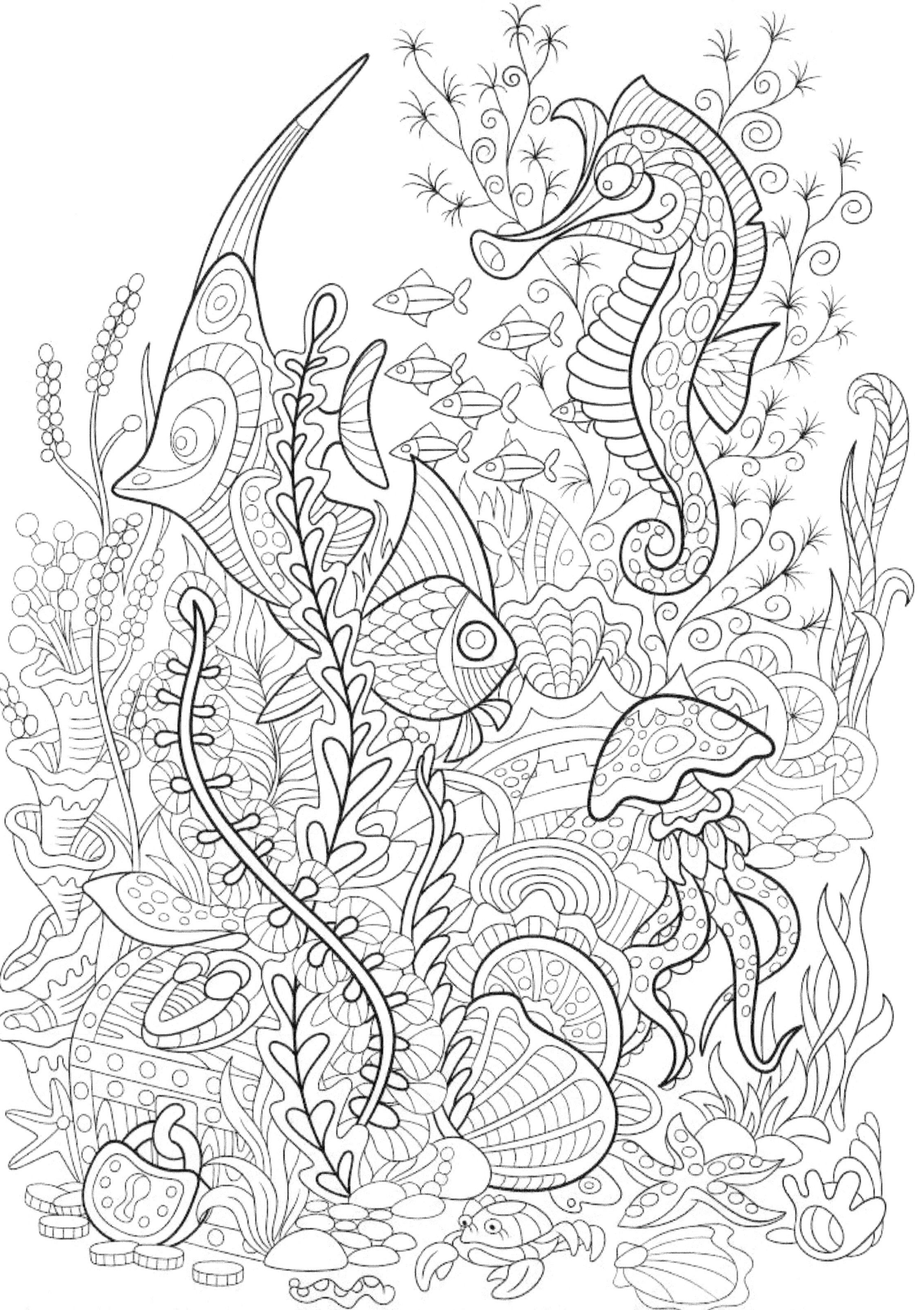

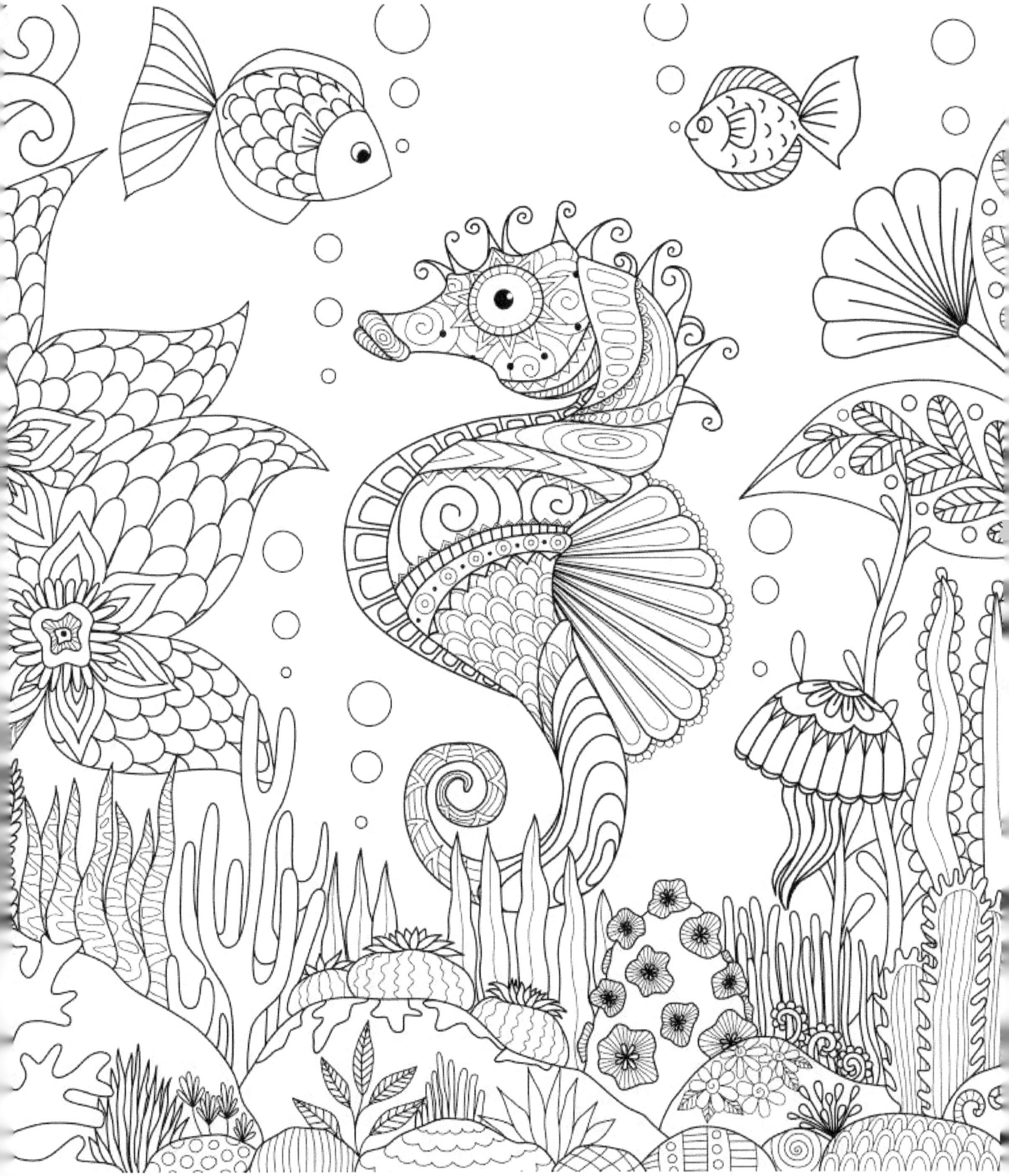

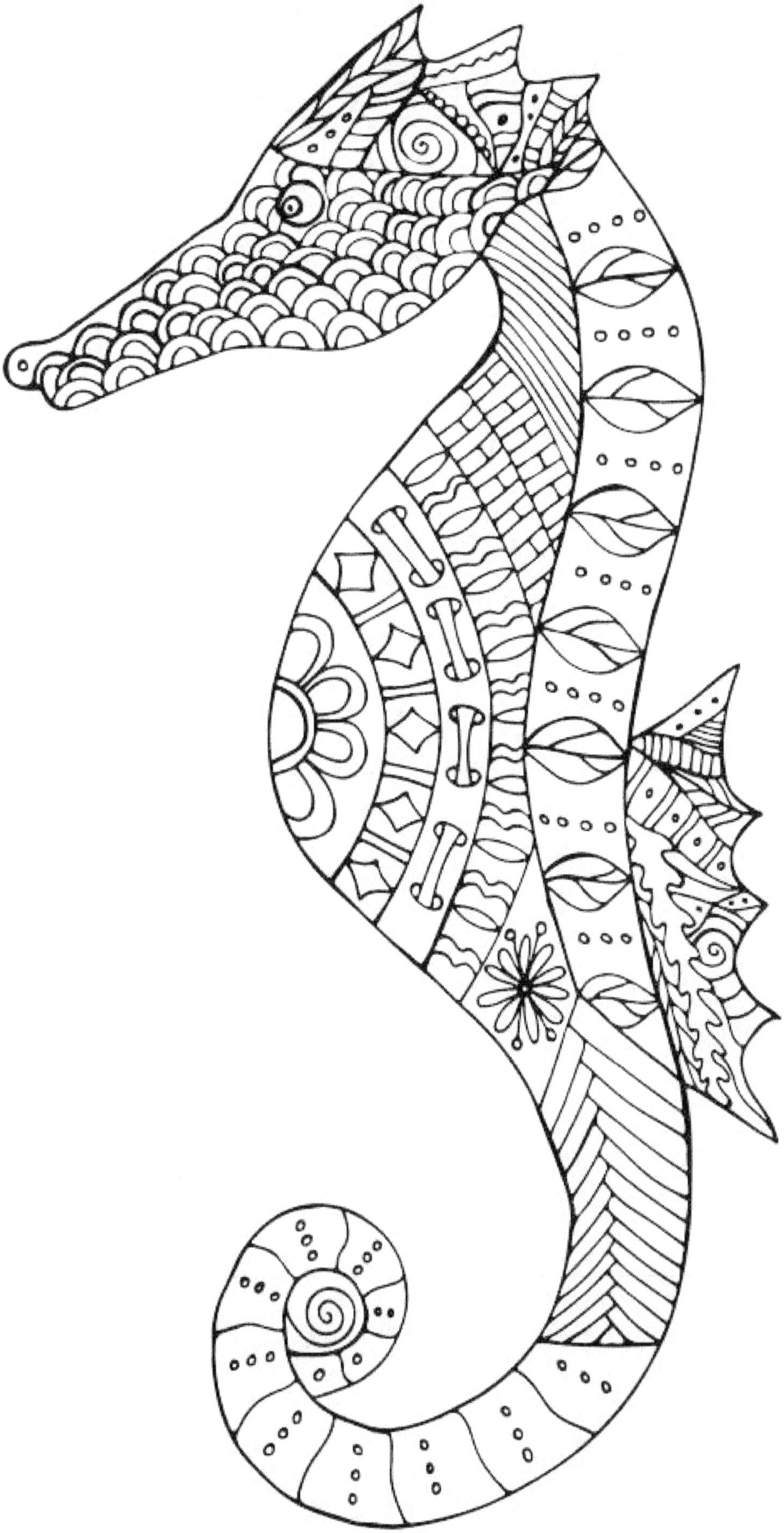

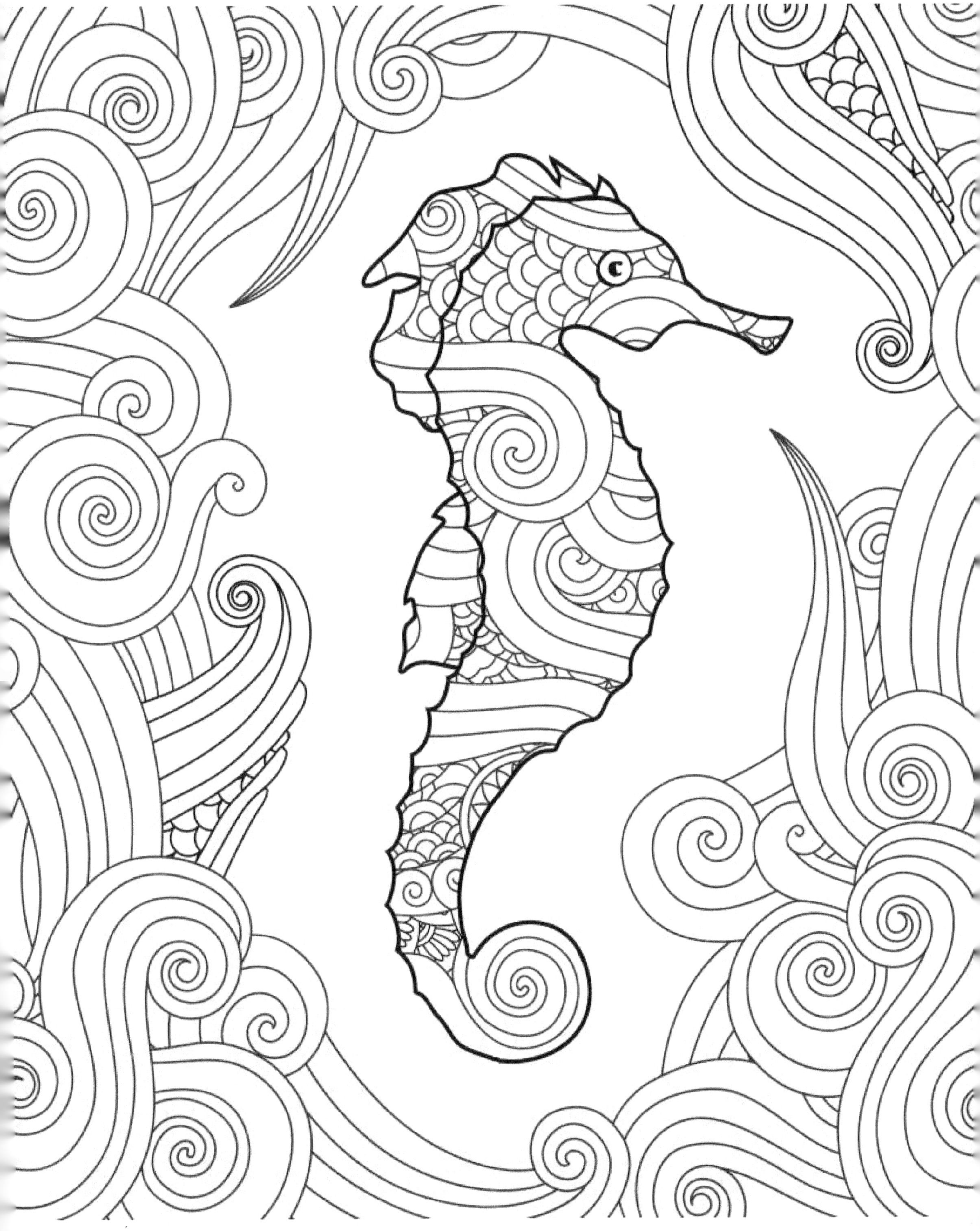

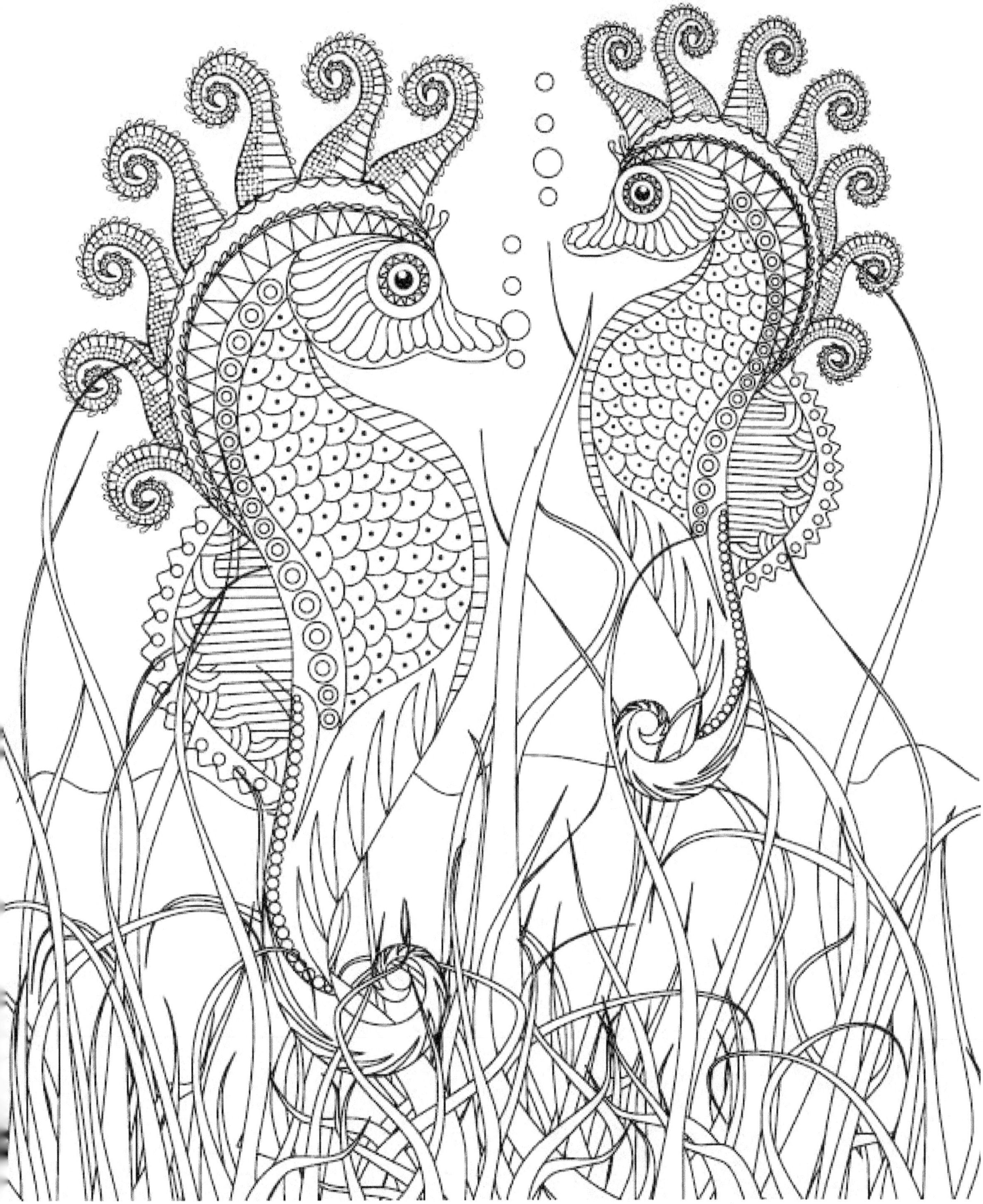

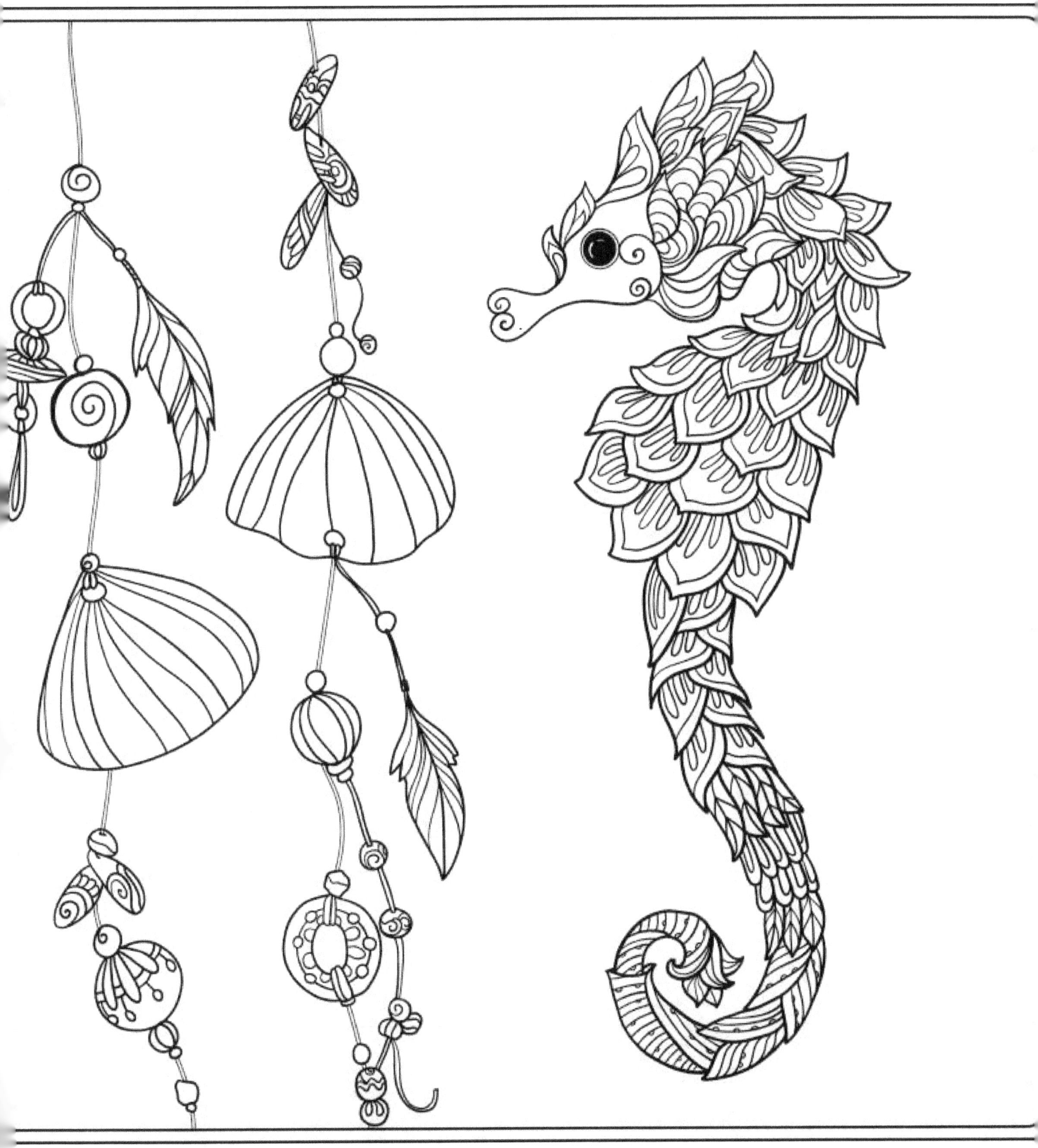

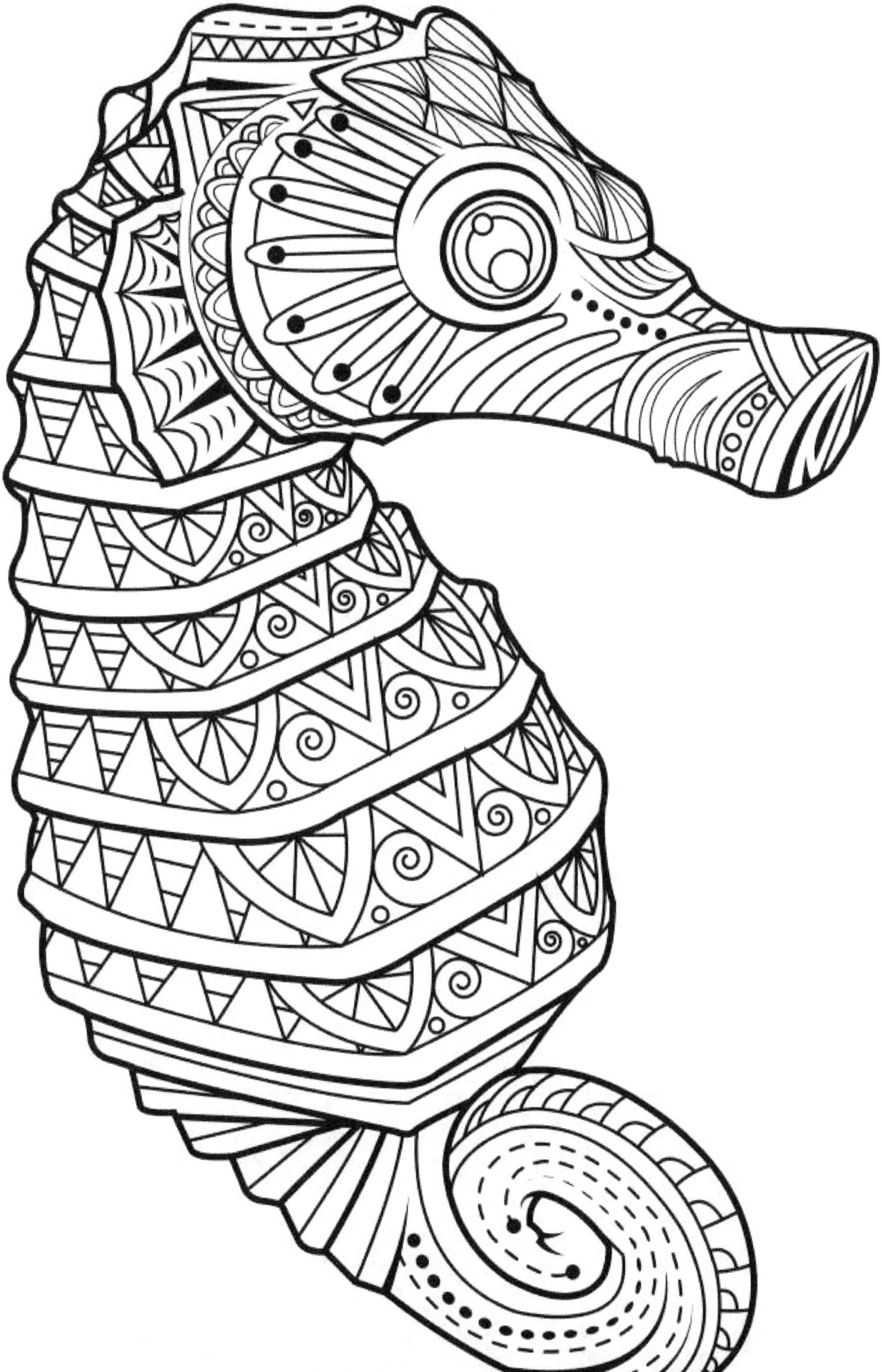

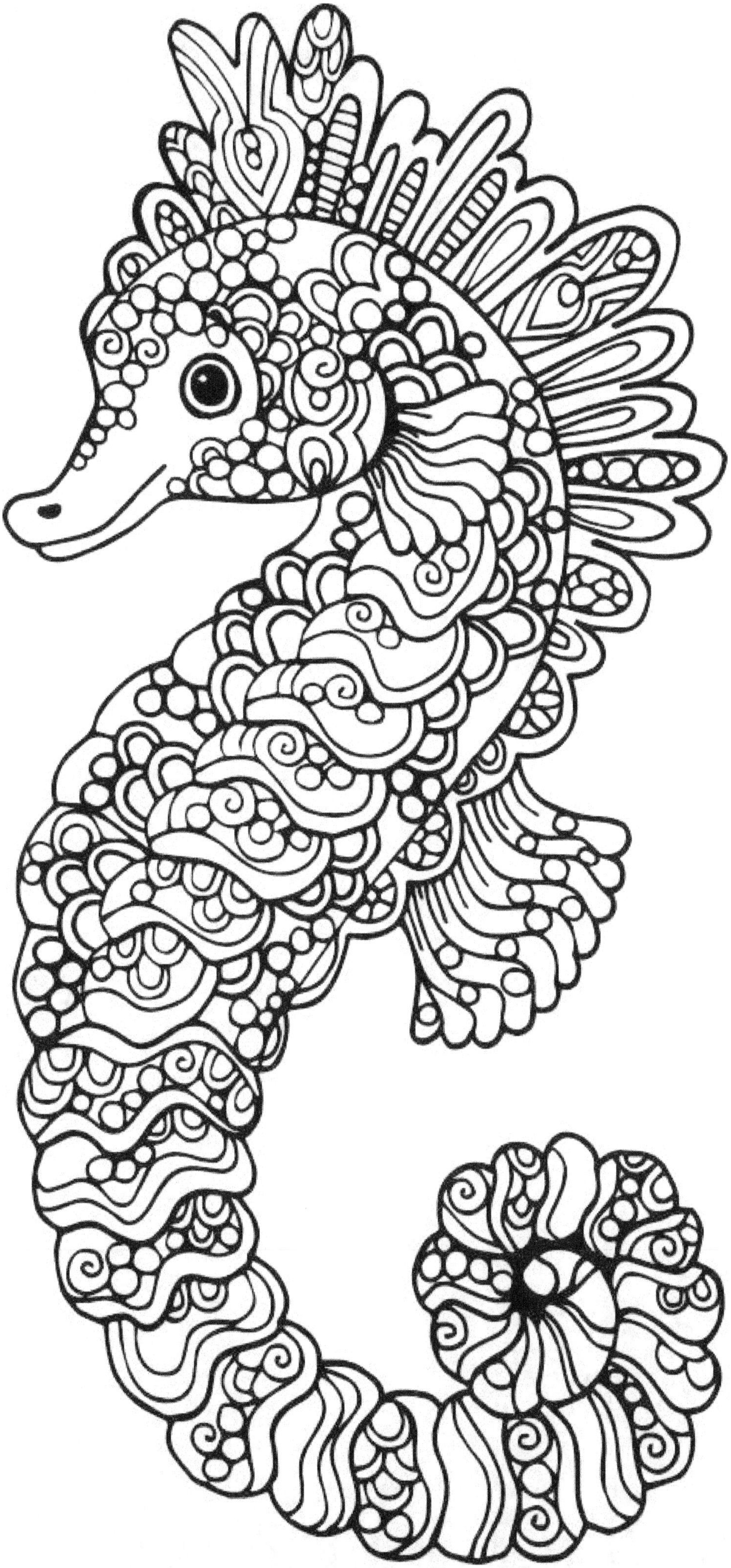

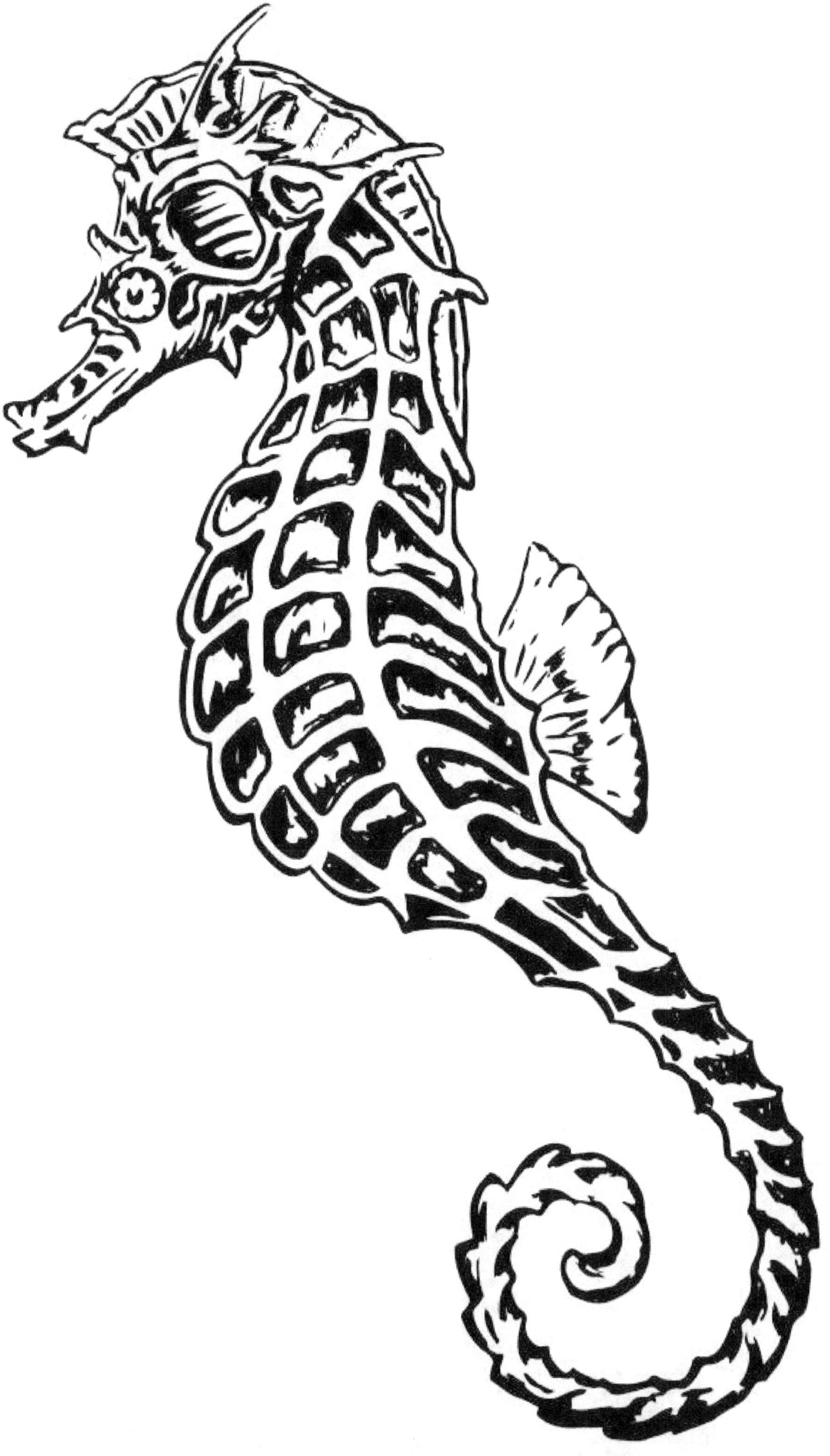

Surprise Bonus Ships and Octopus Coloring Pages to Enjoy

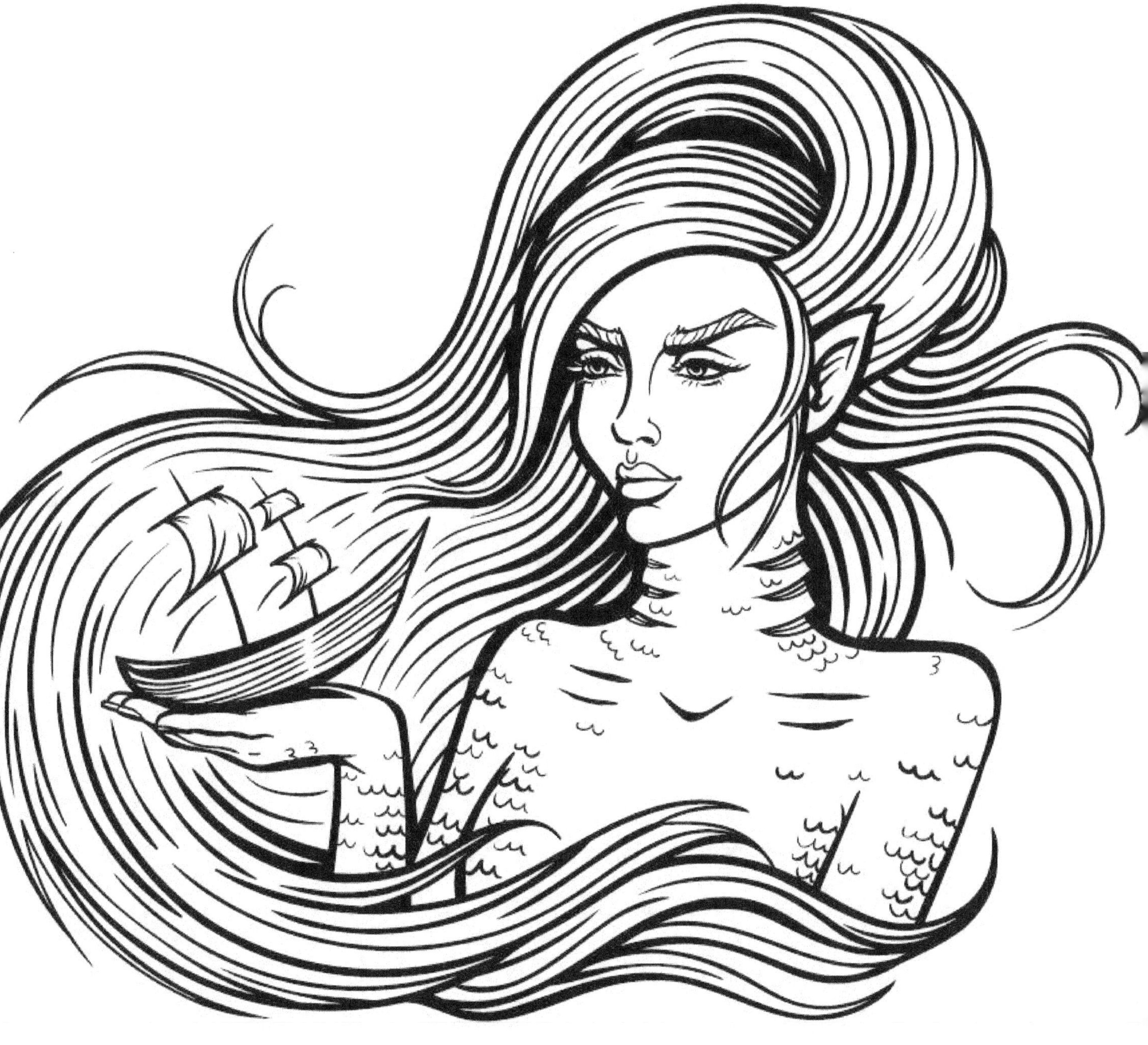

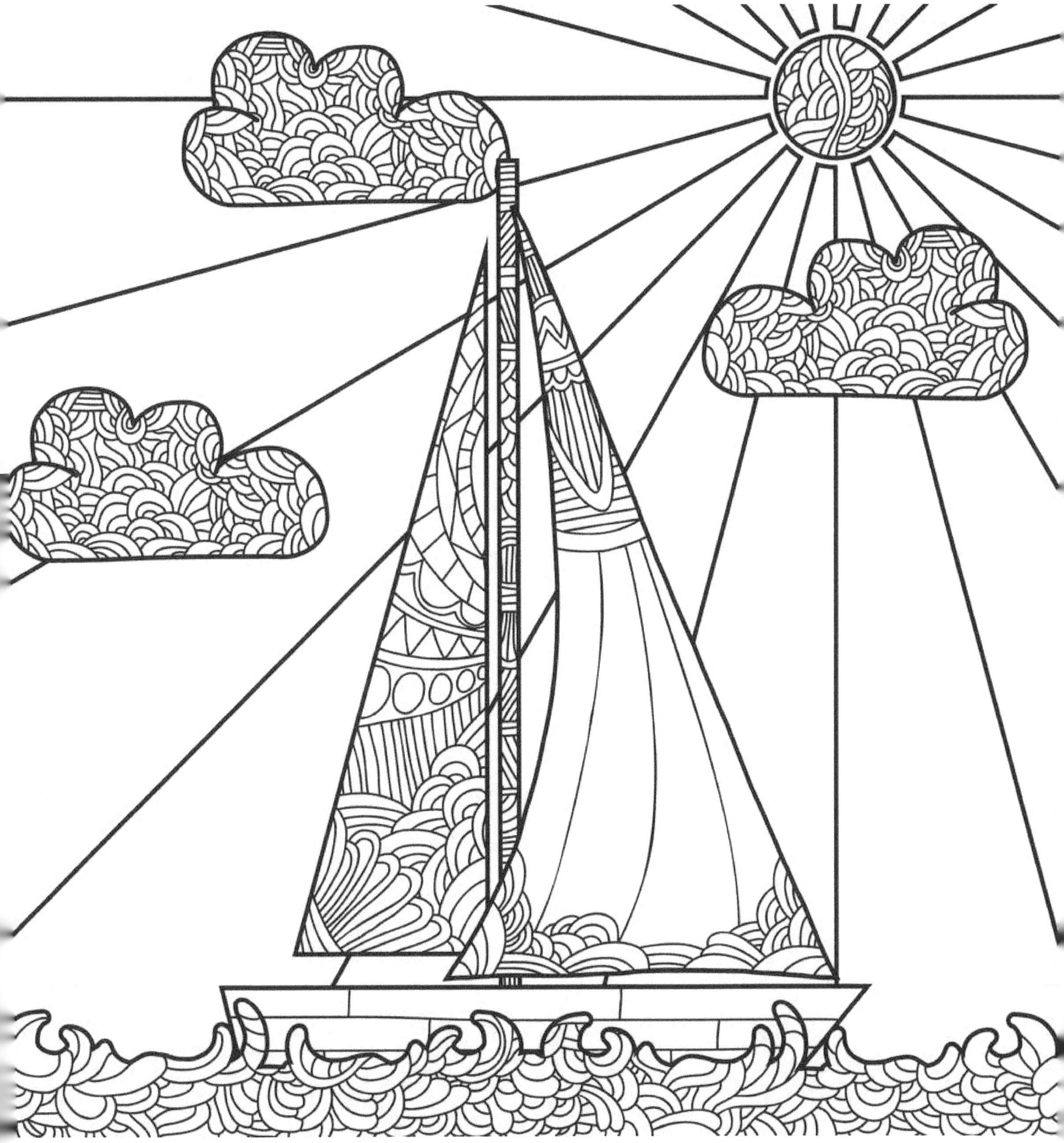

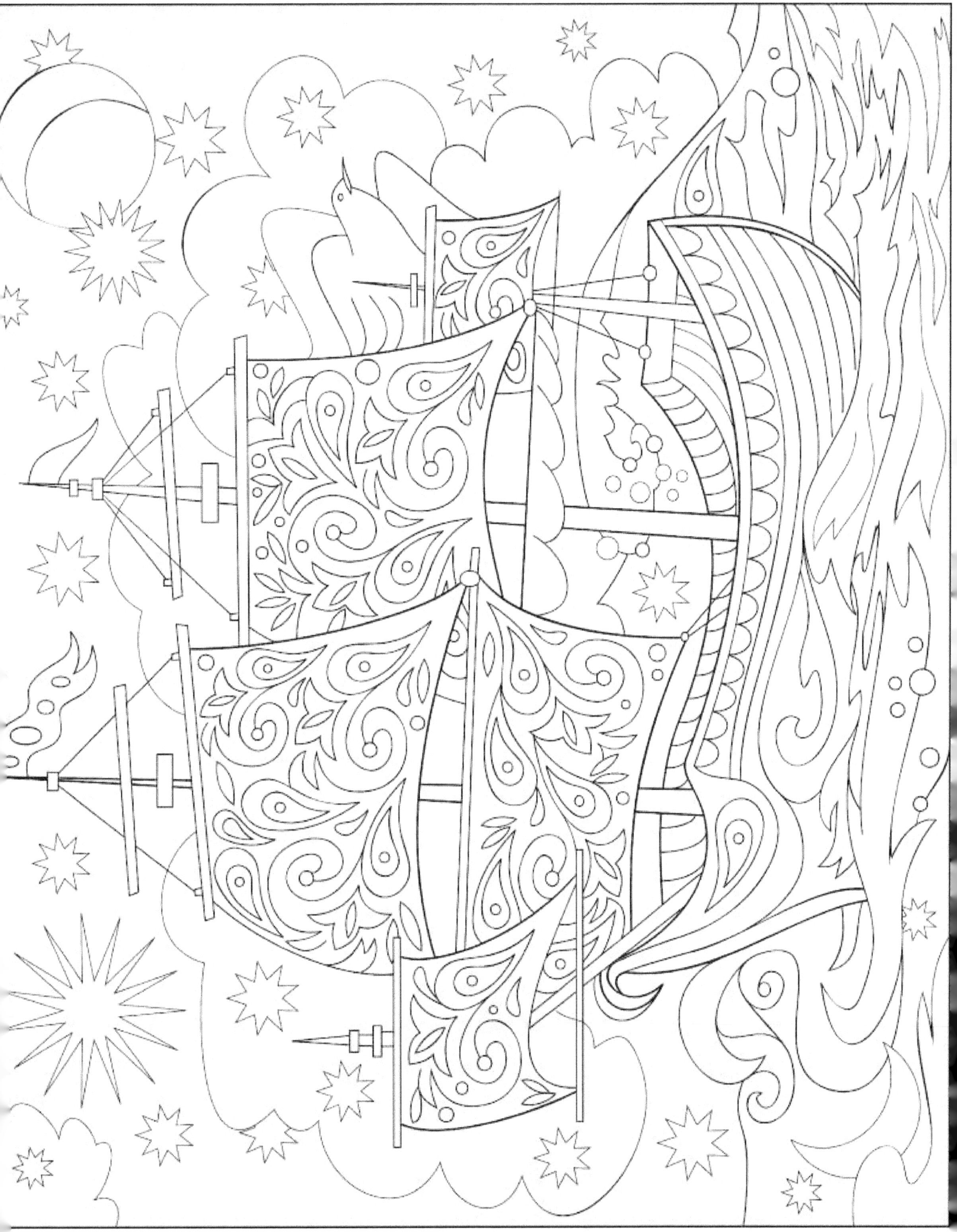

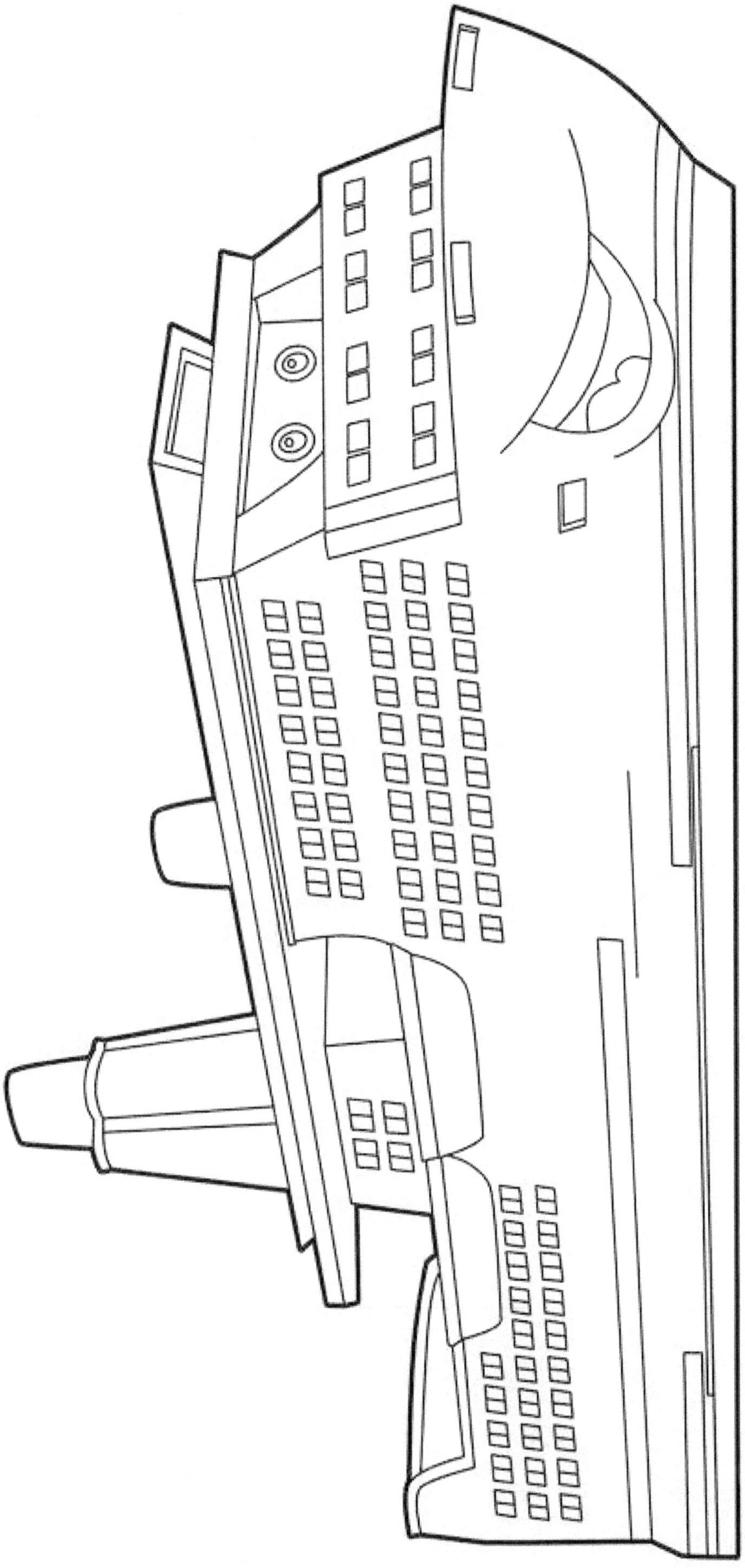

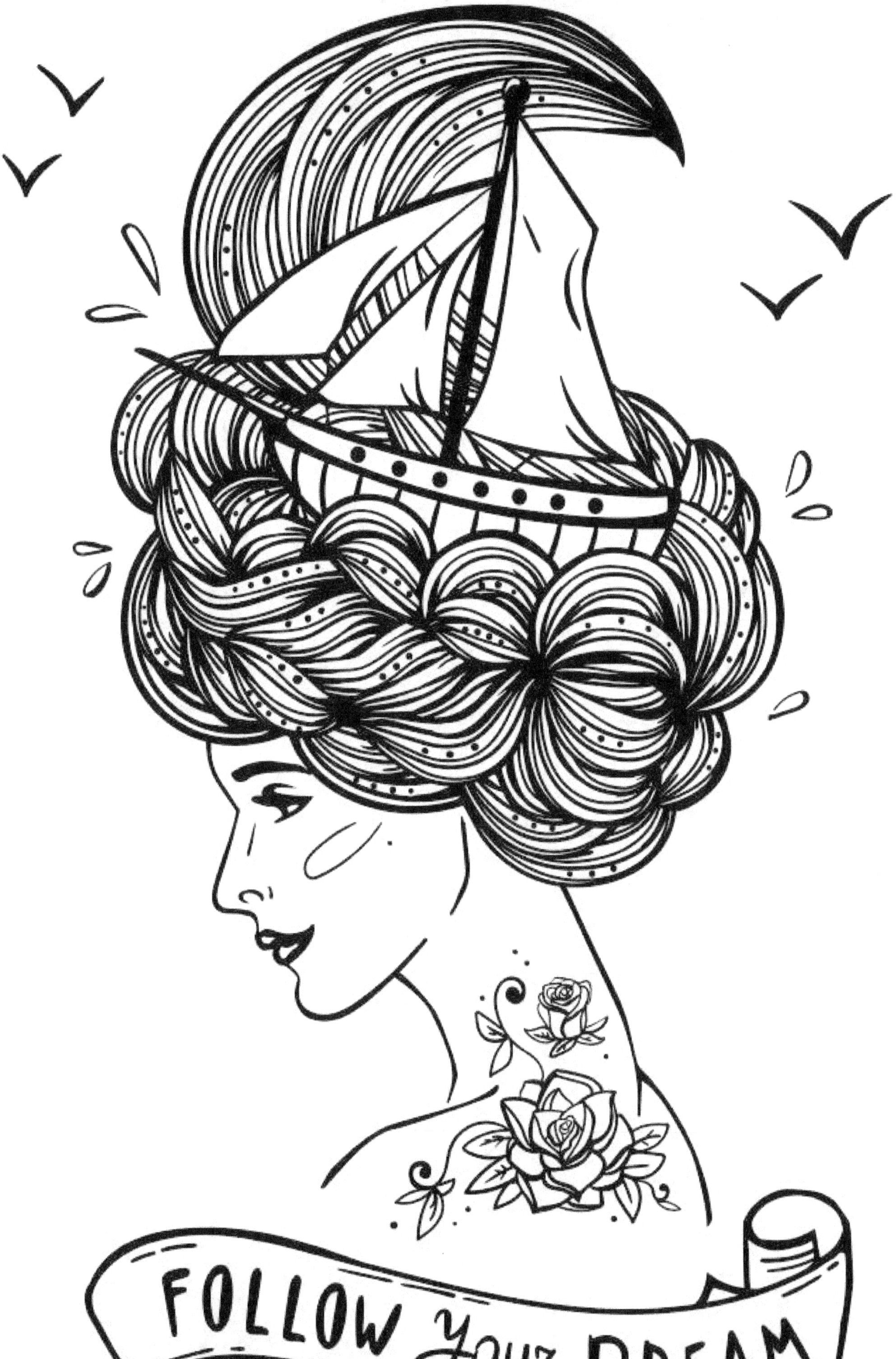
FOLLOW your DREAM

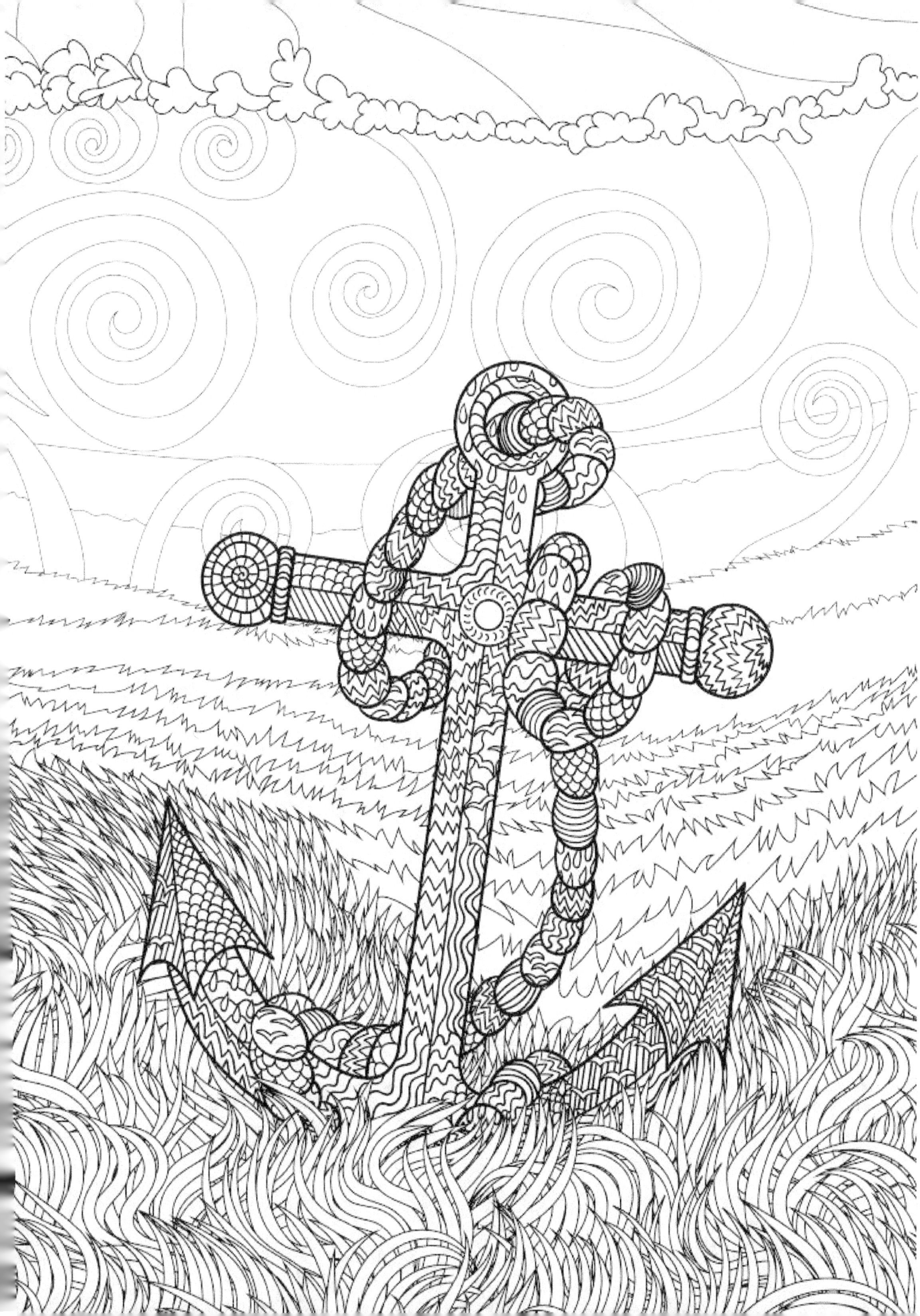

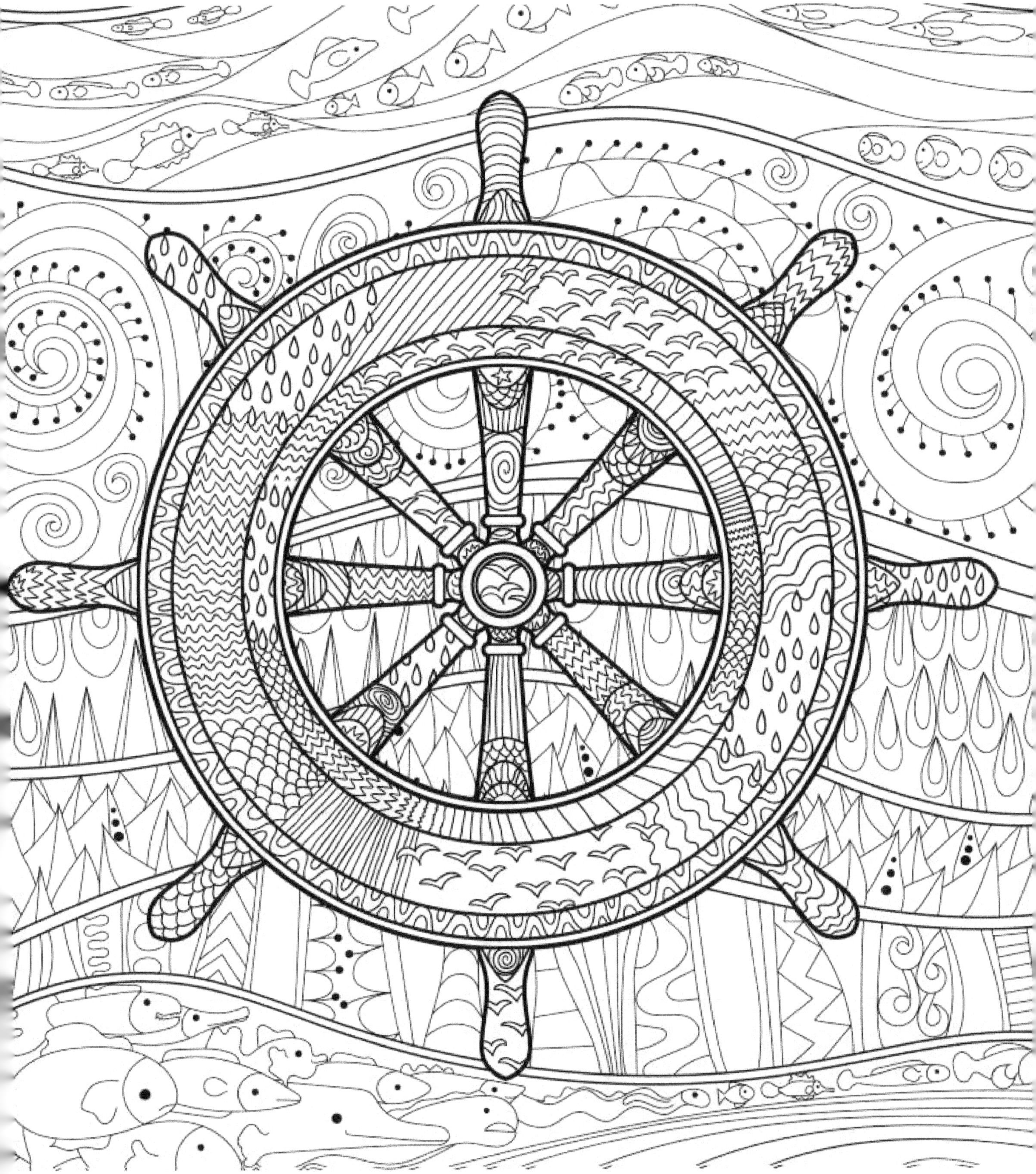

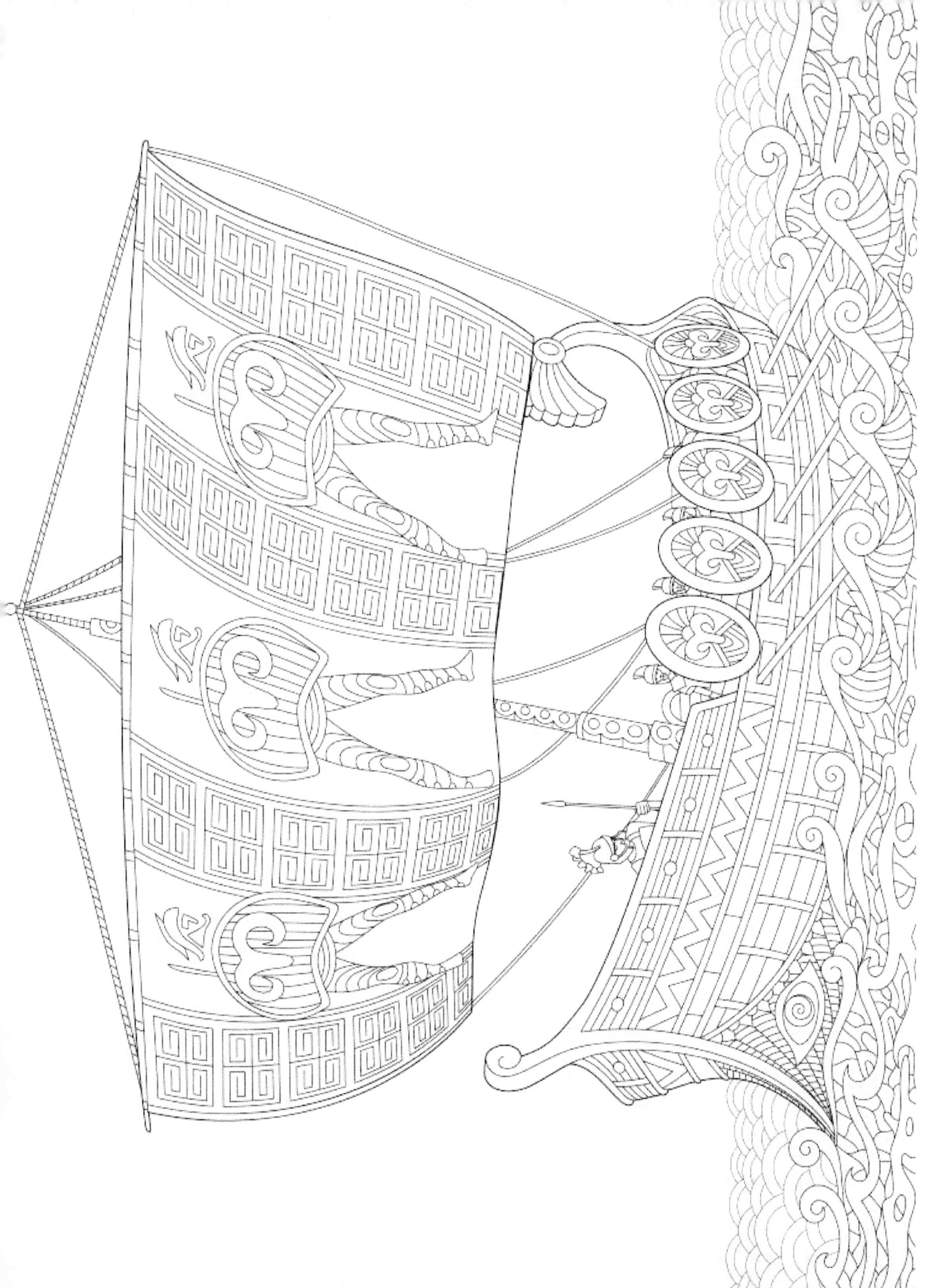

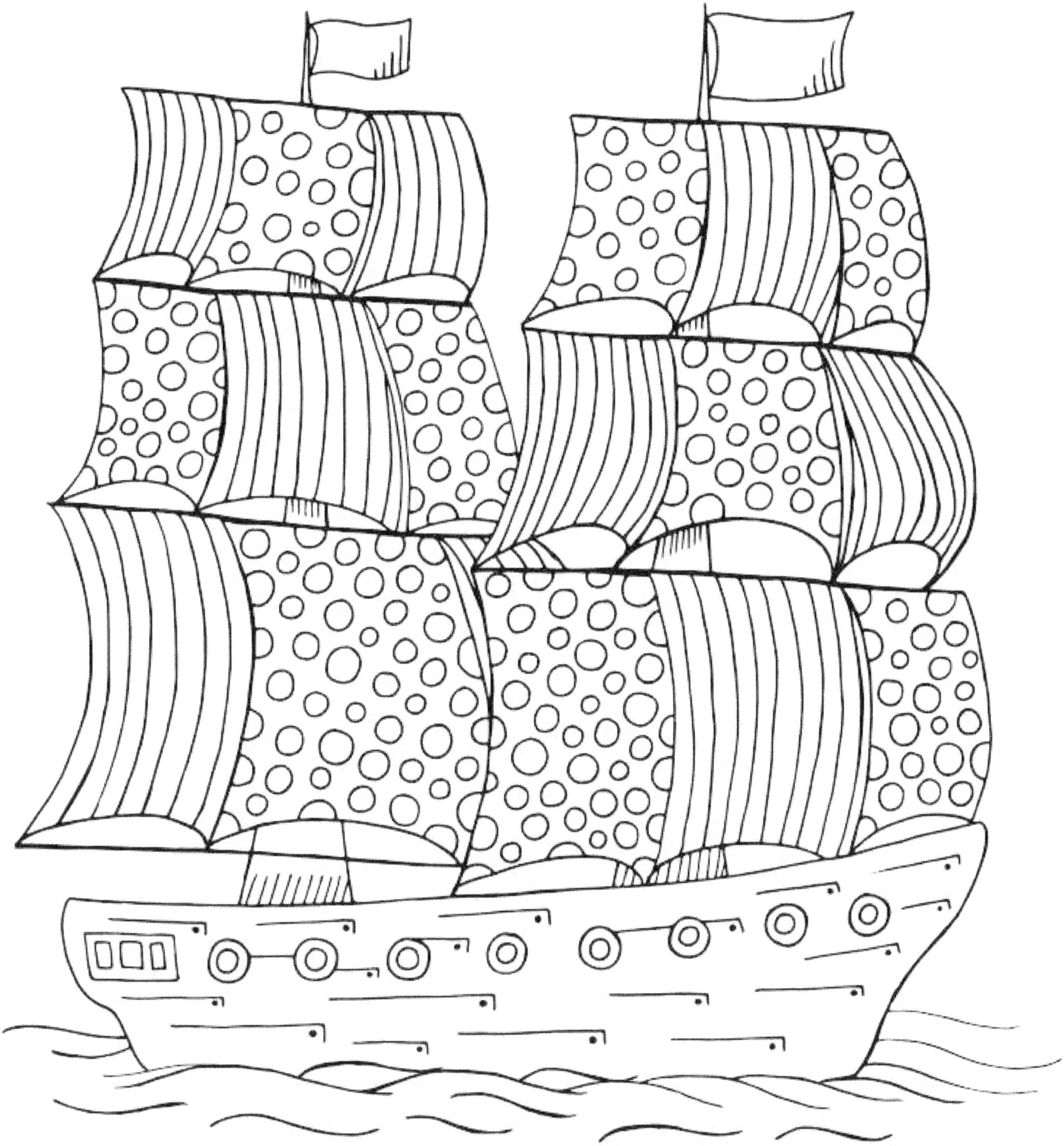

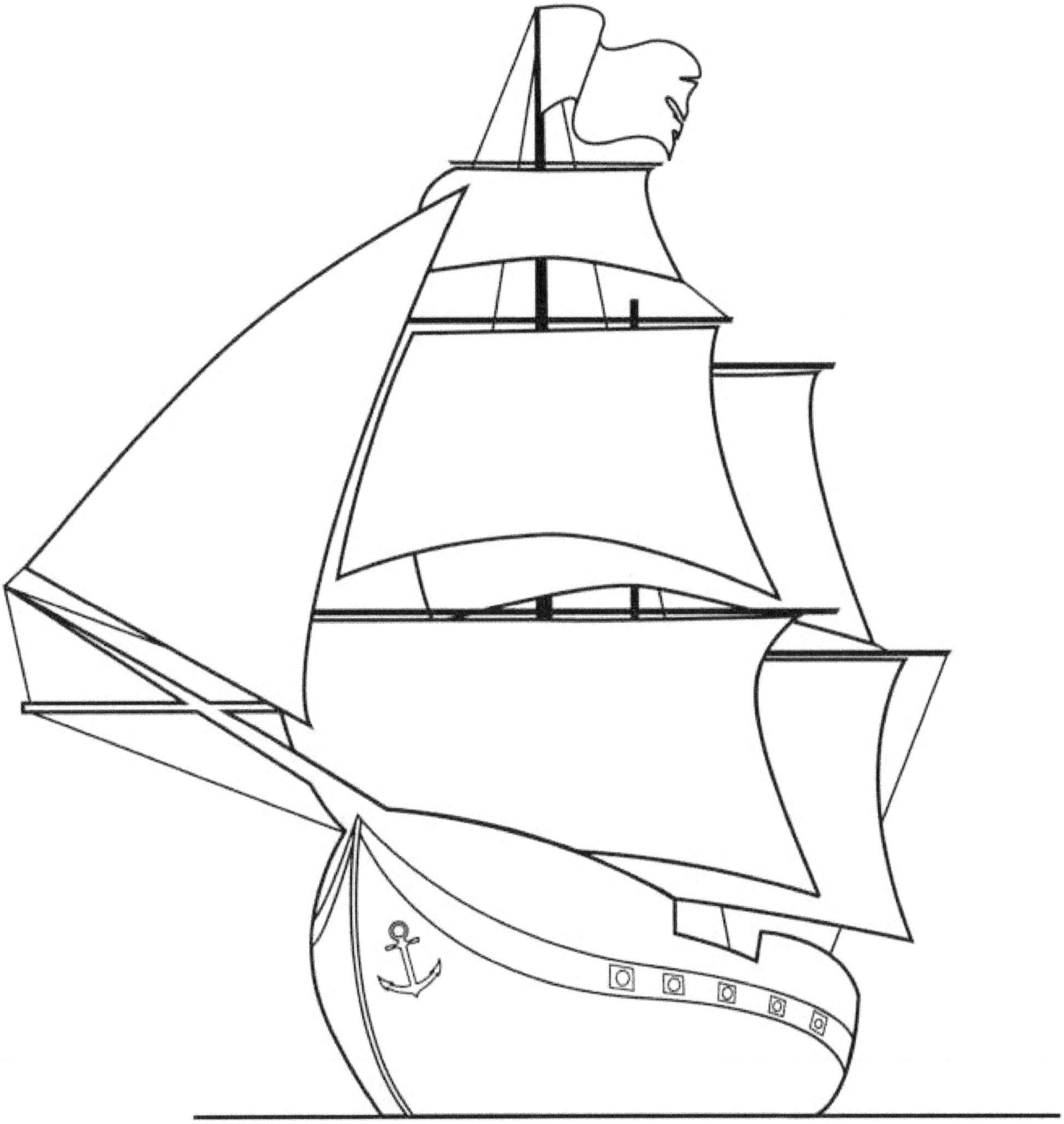

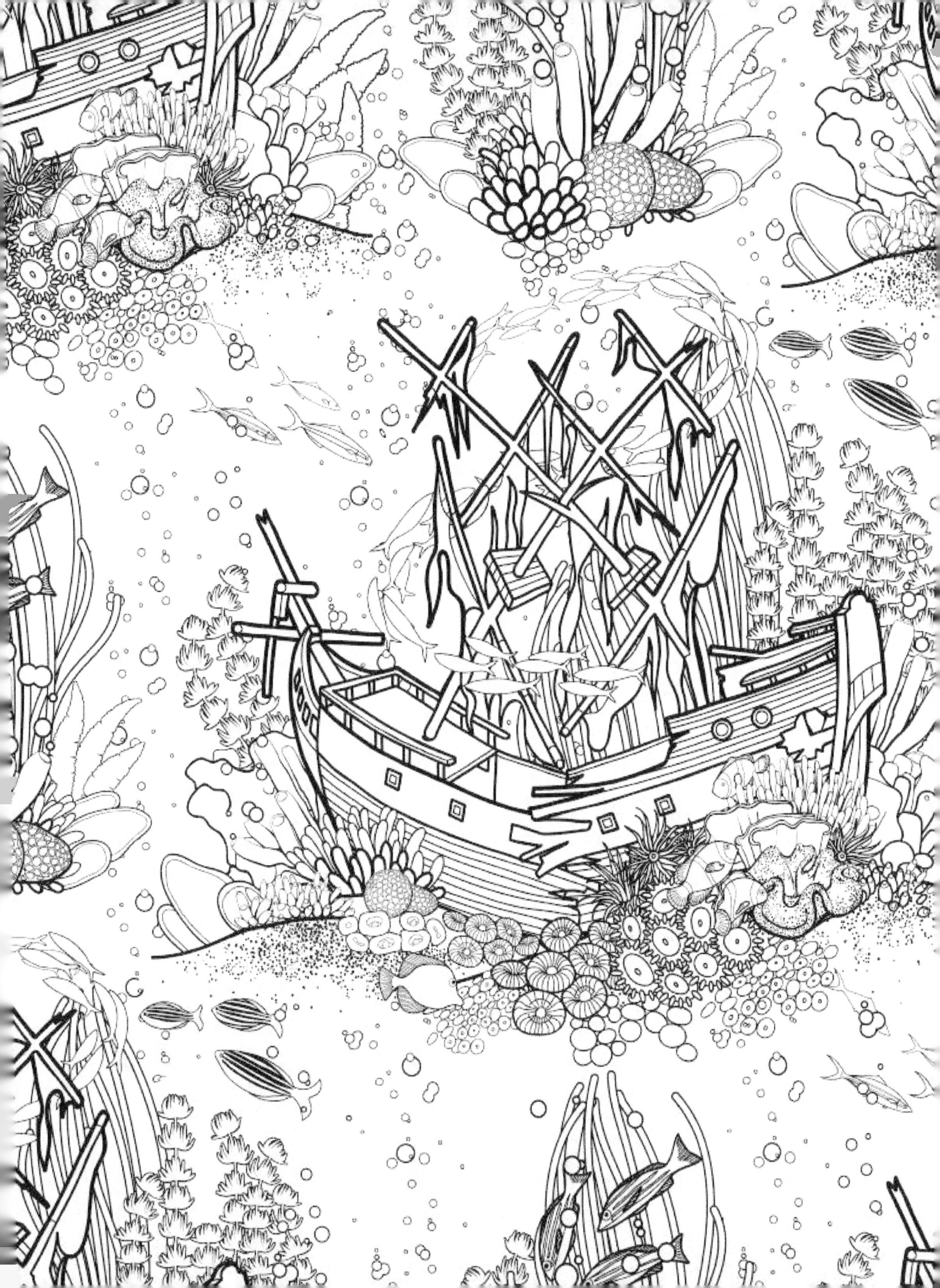

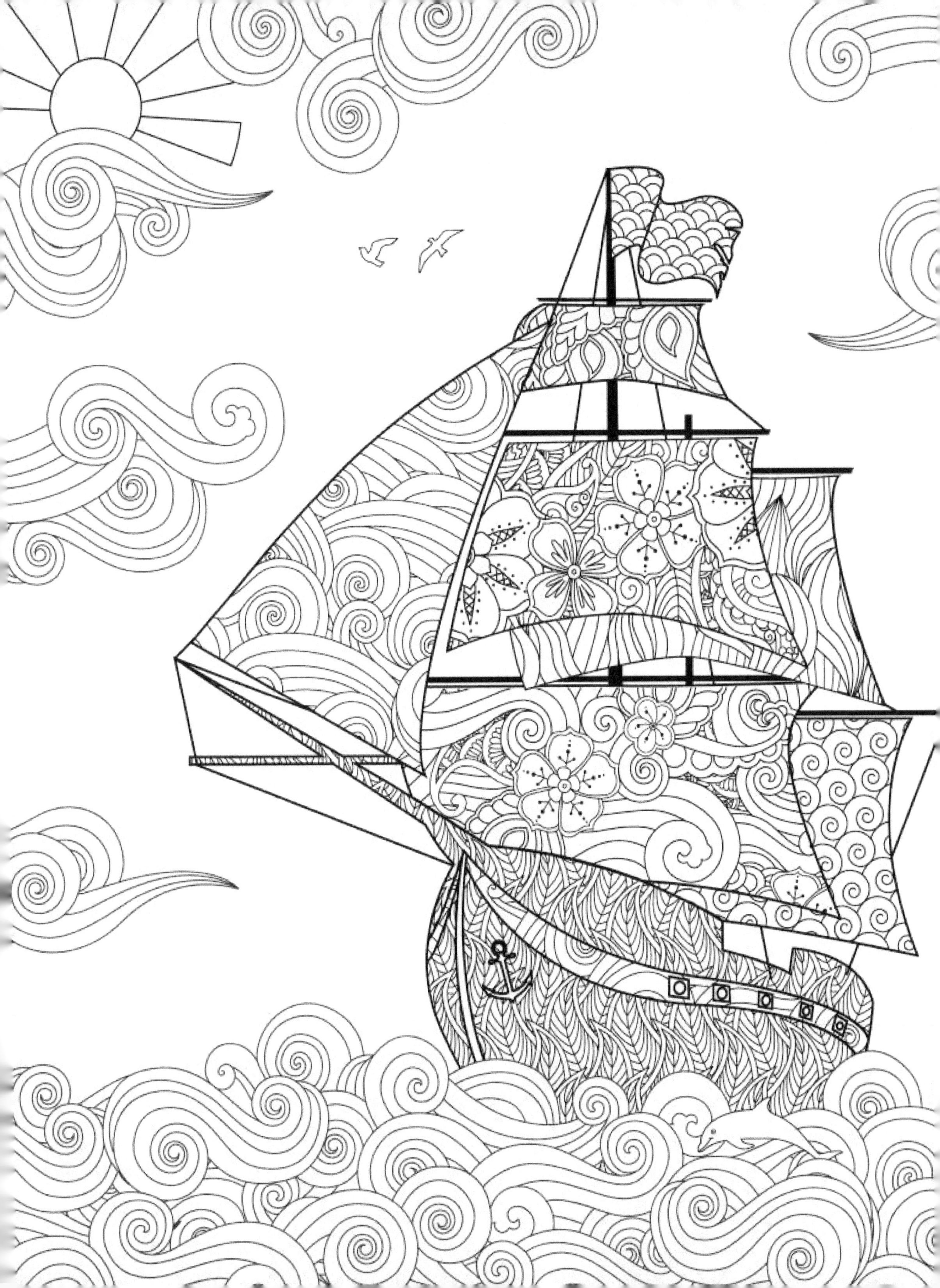

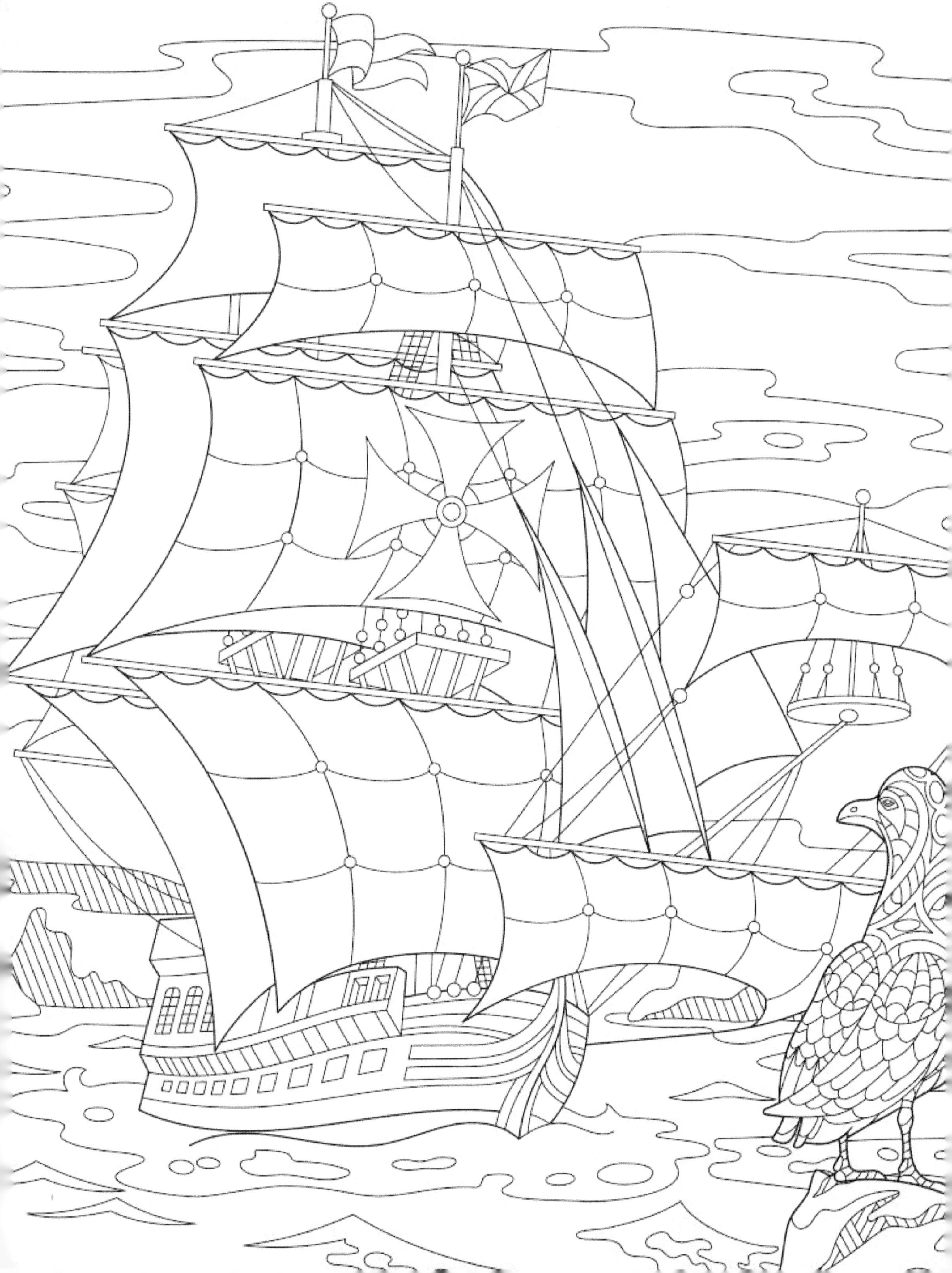

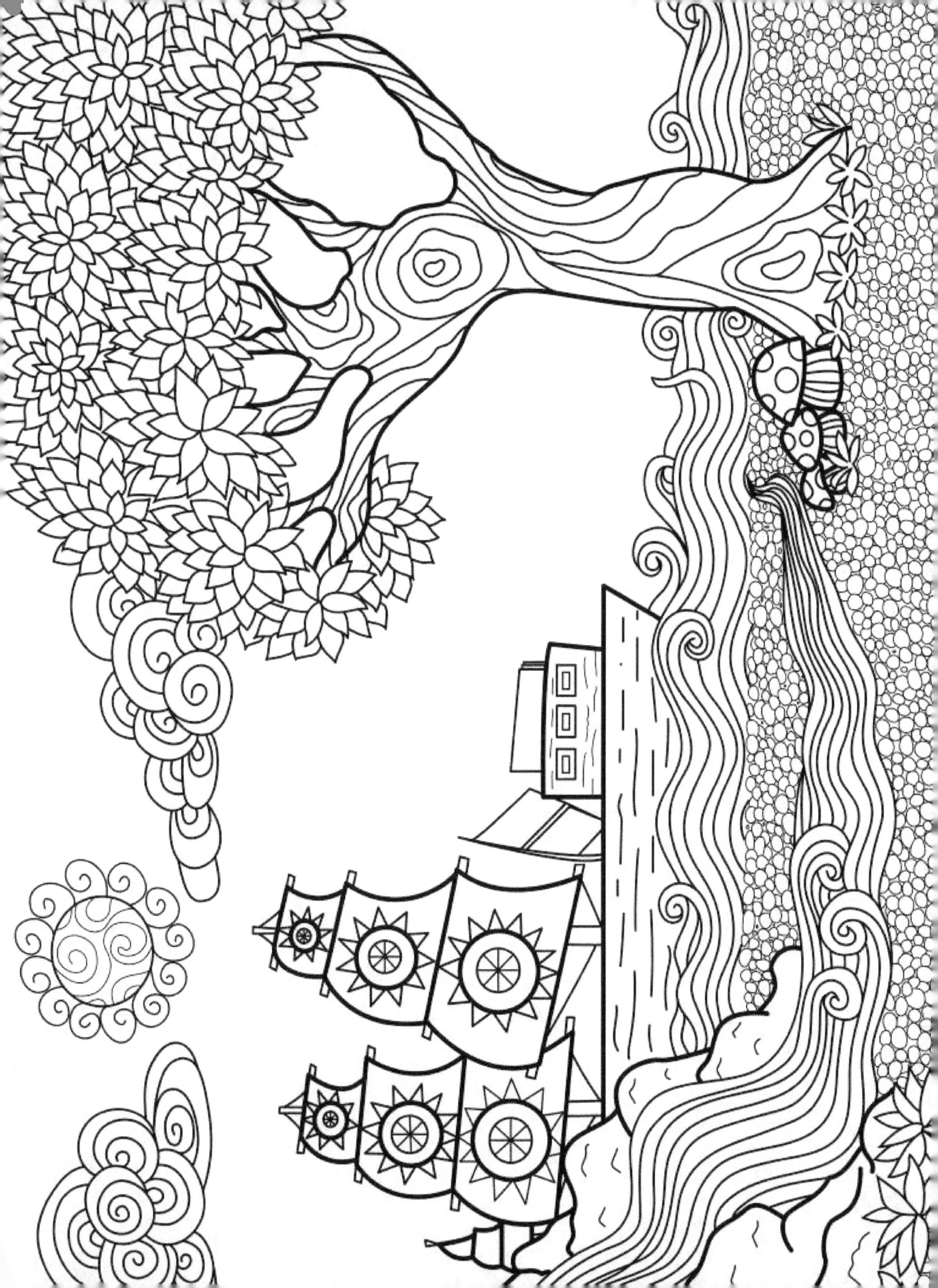

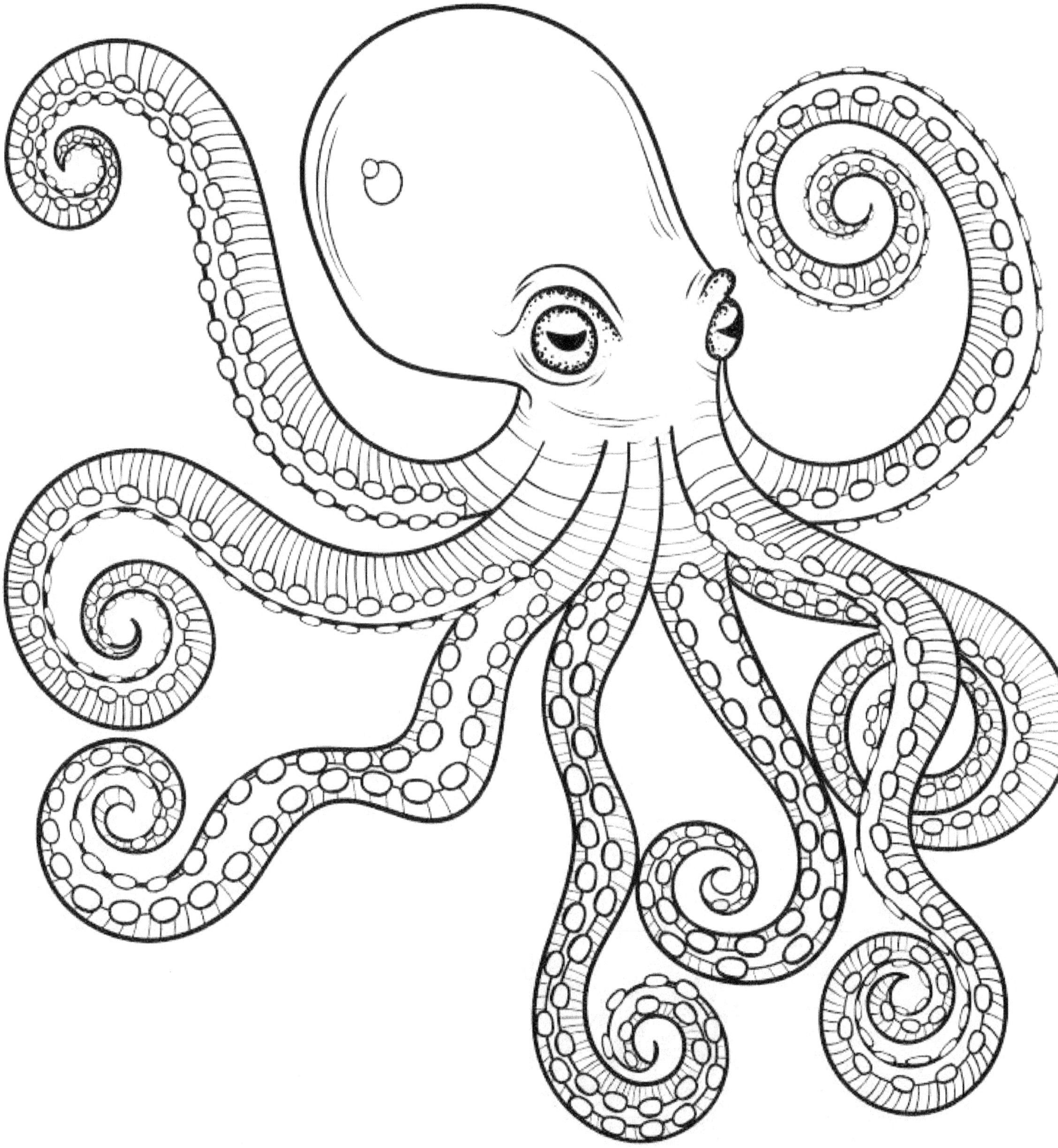

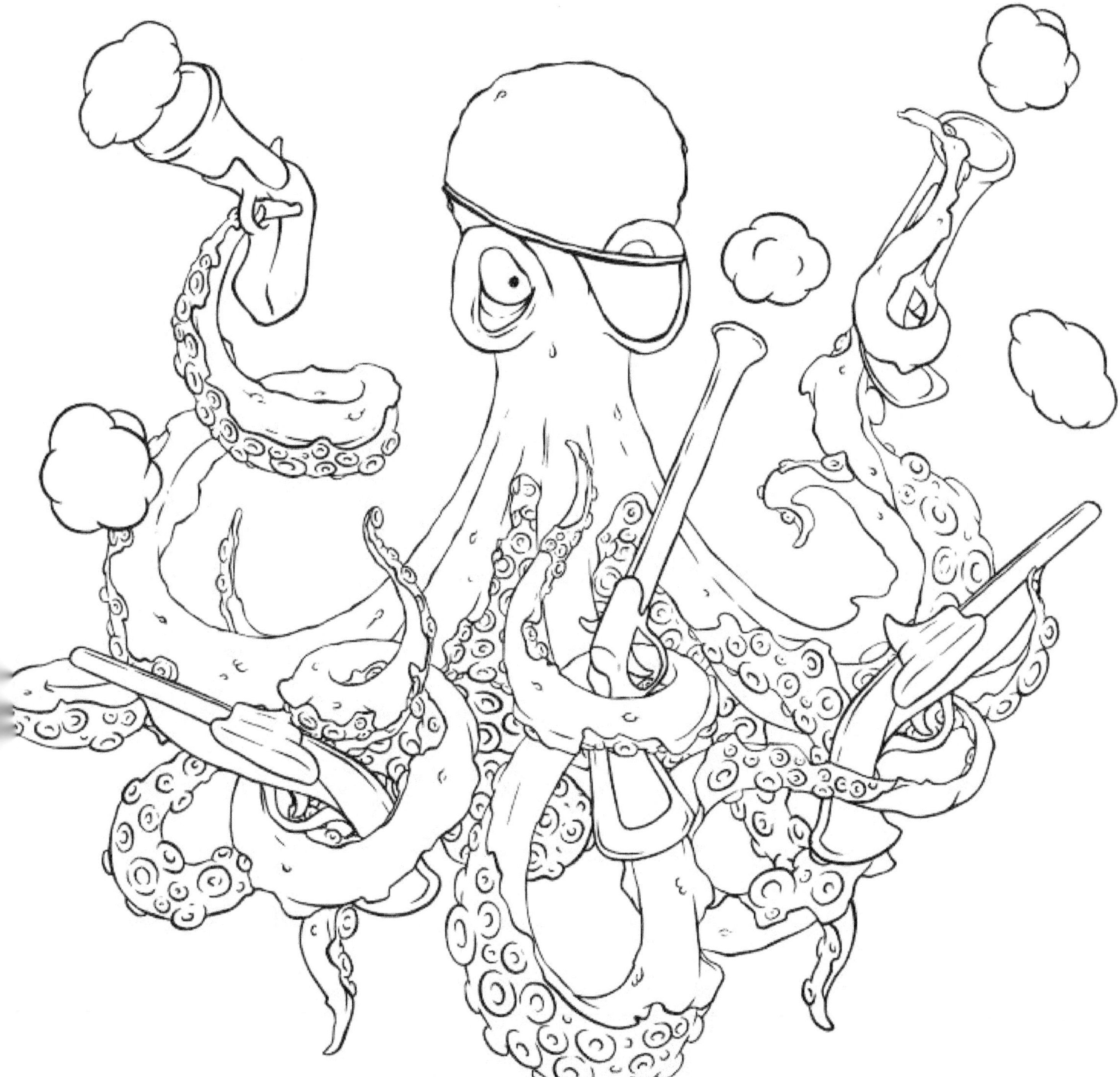

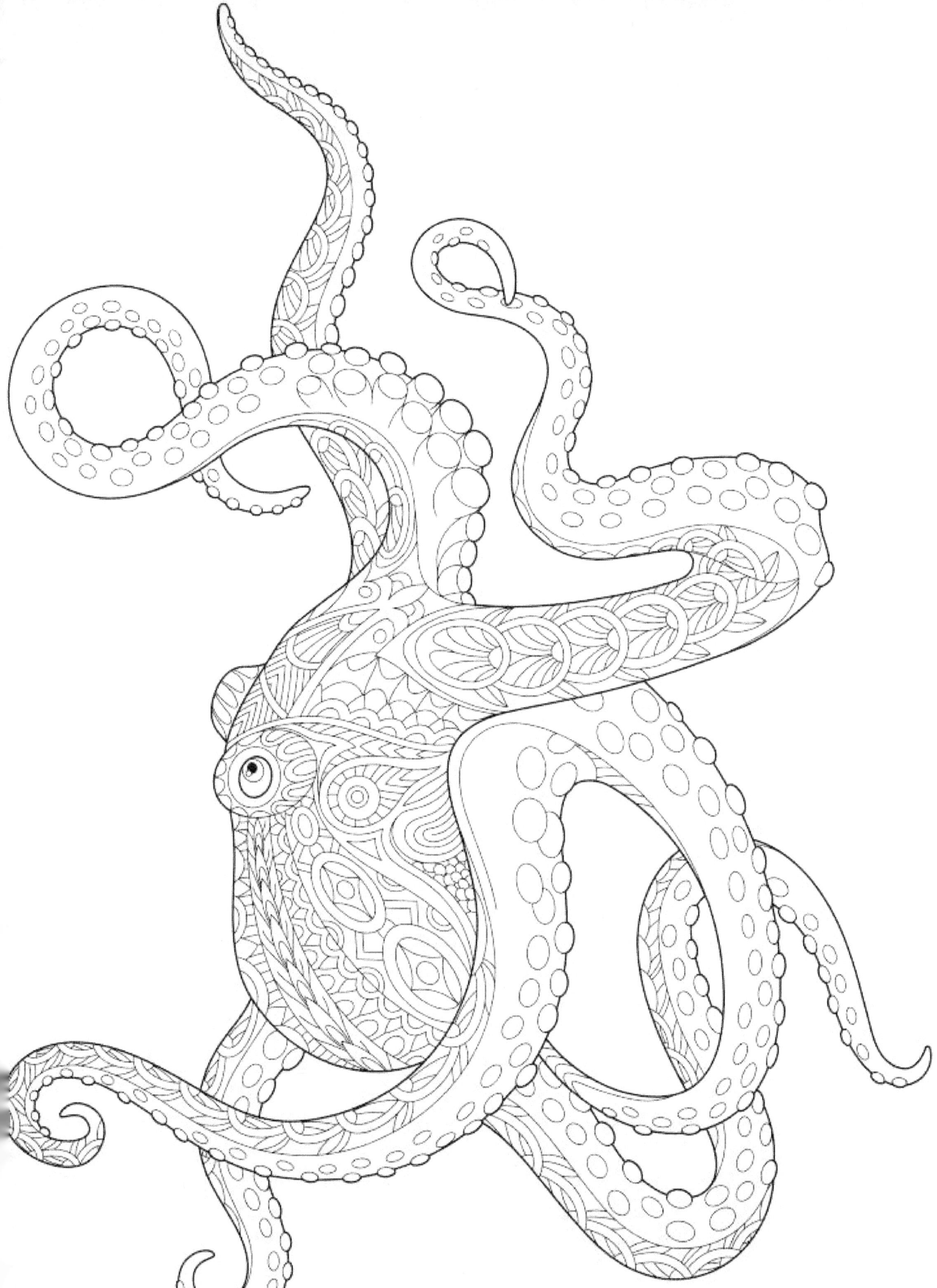

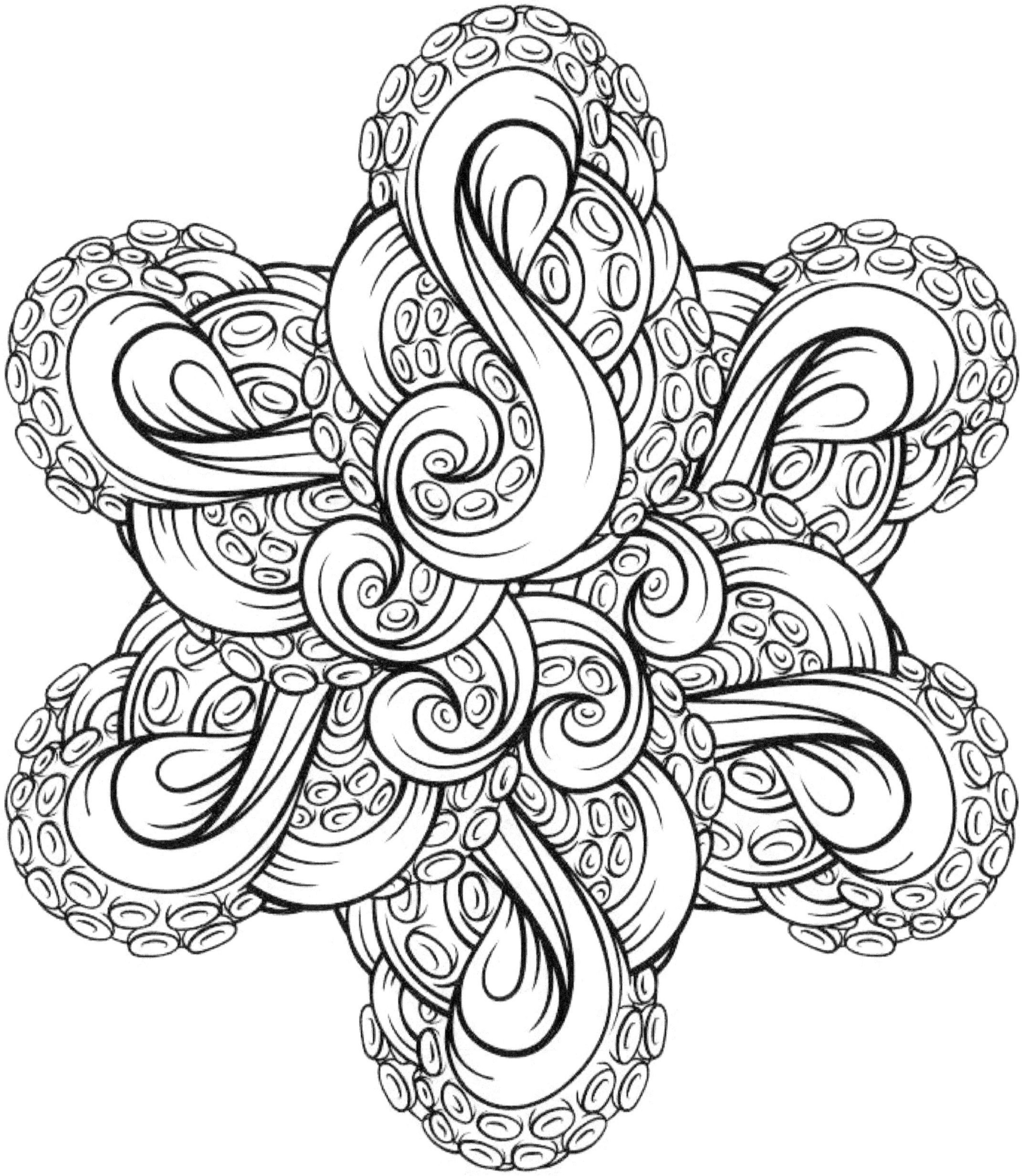

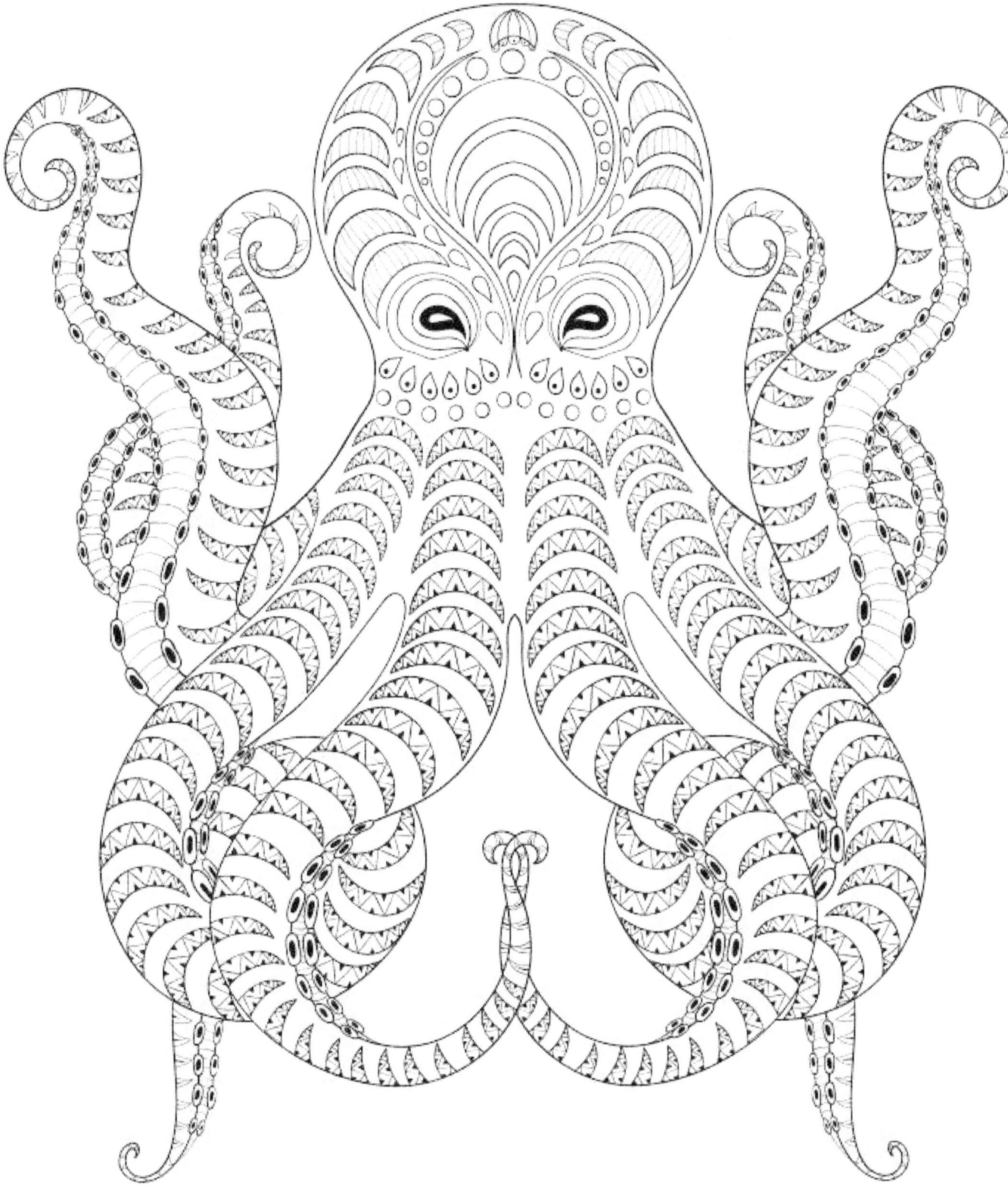

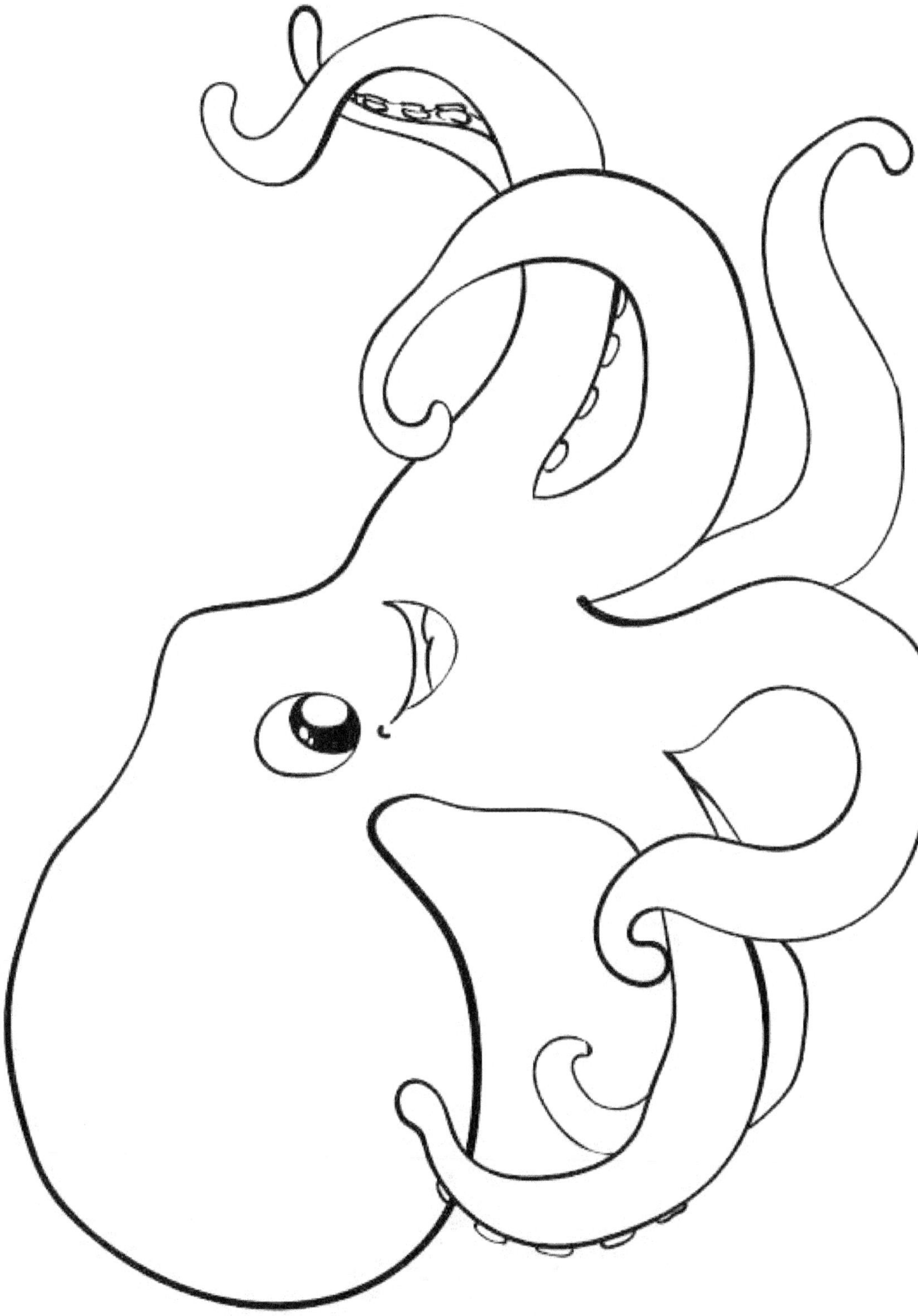

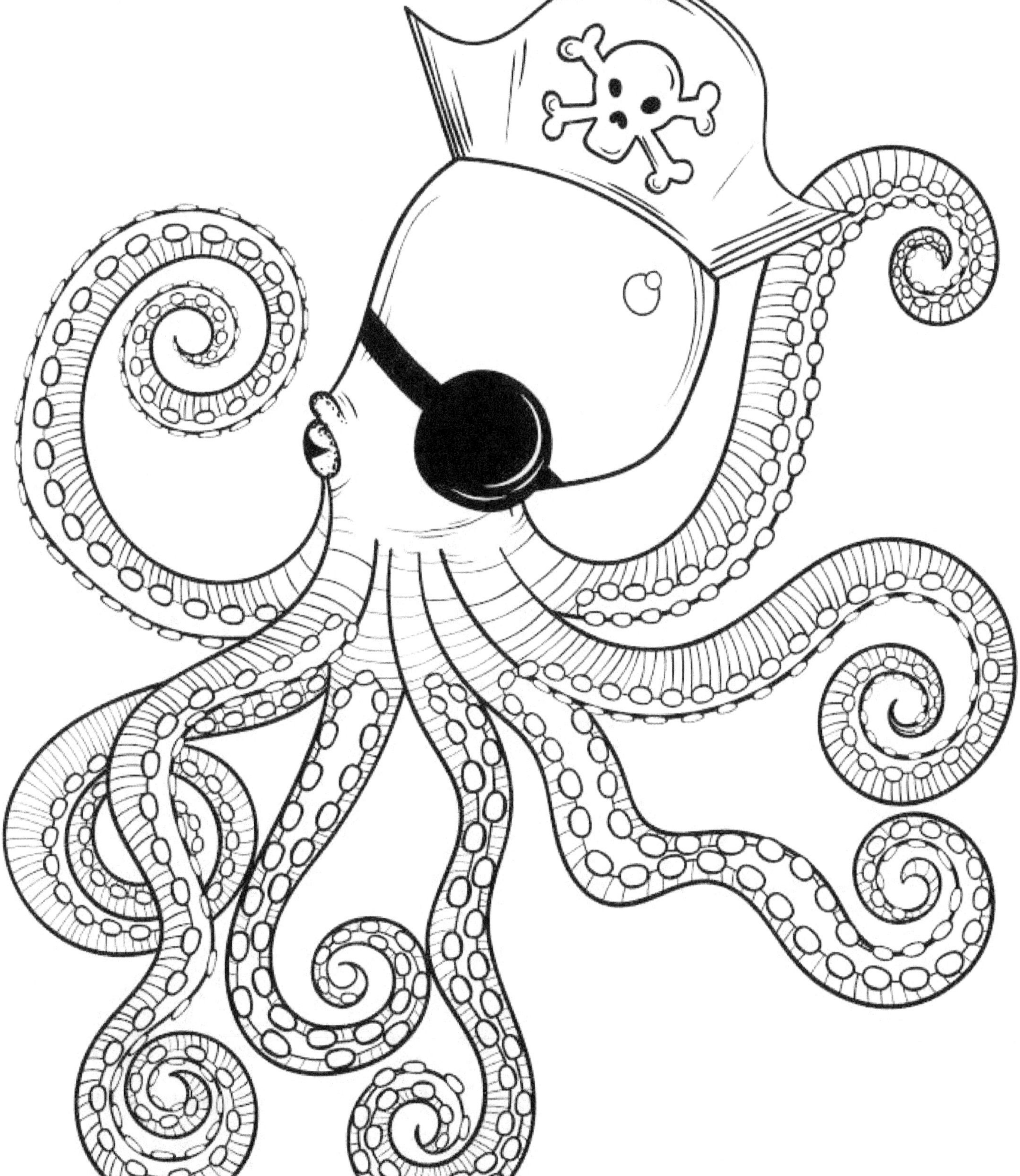

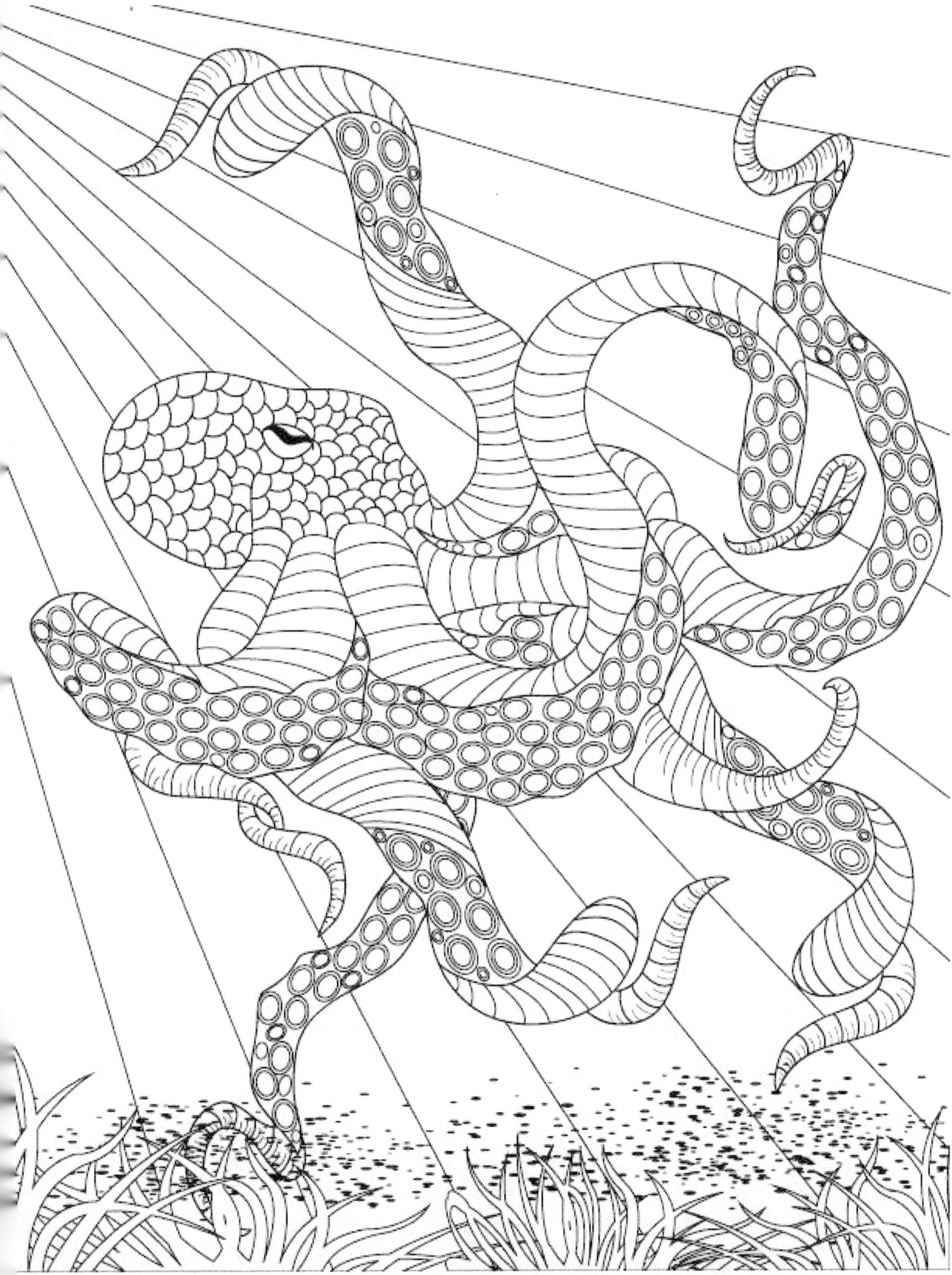

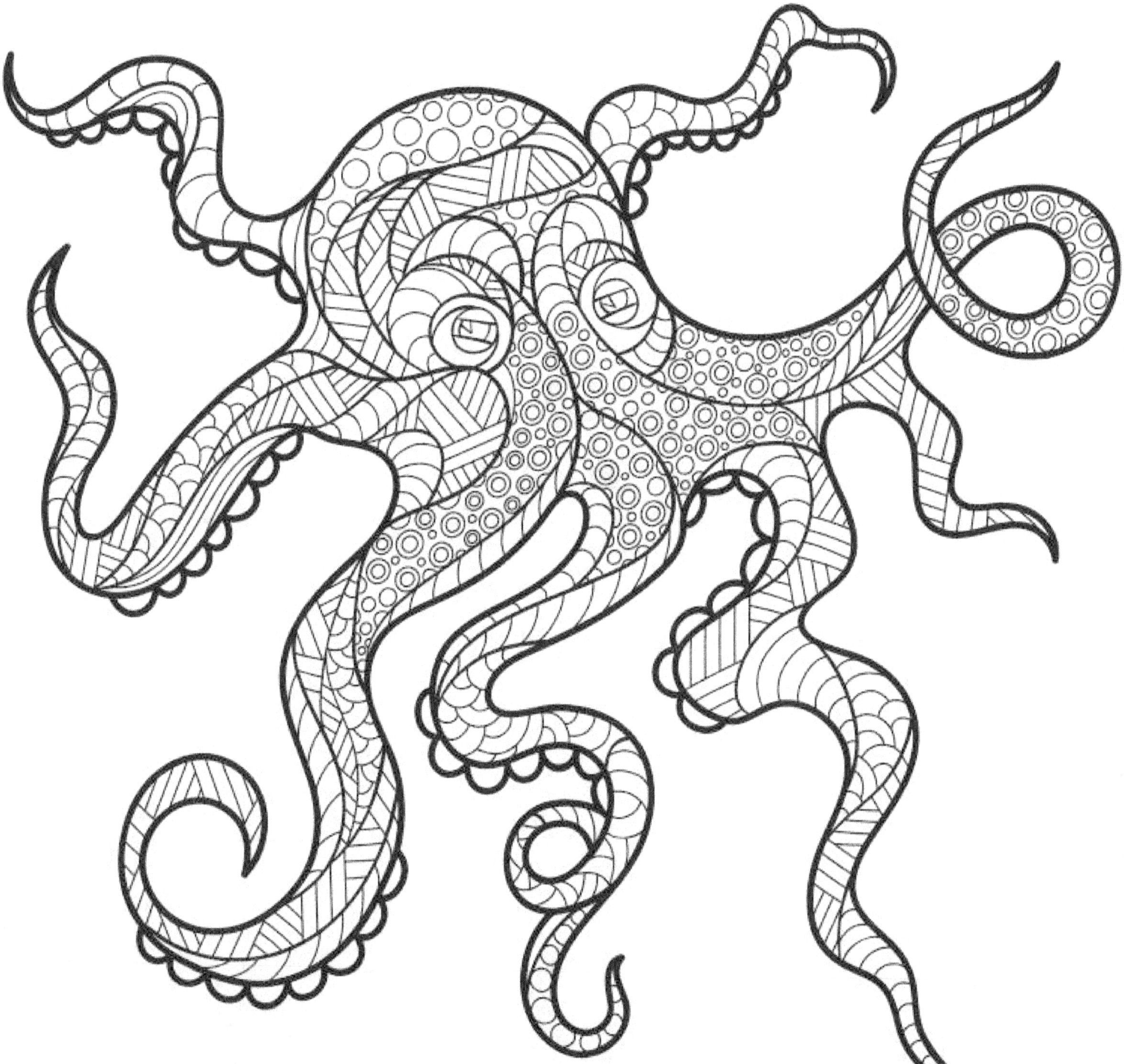

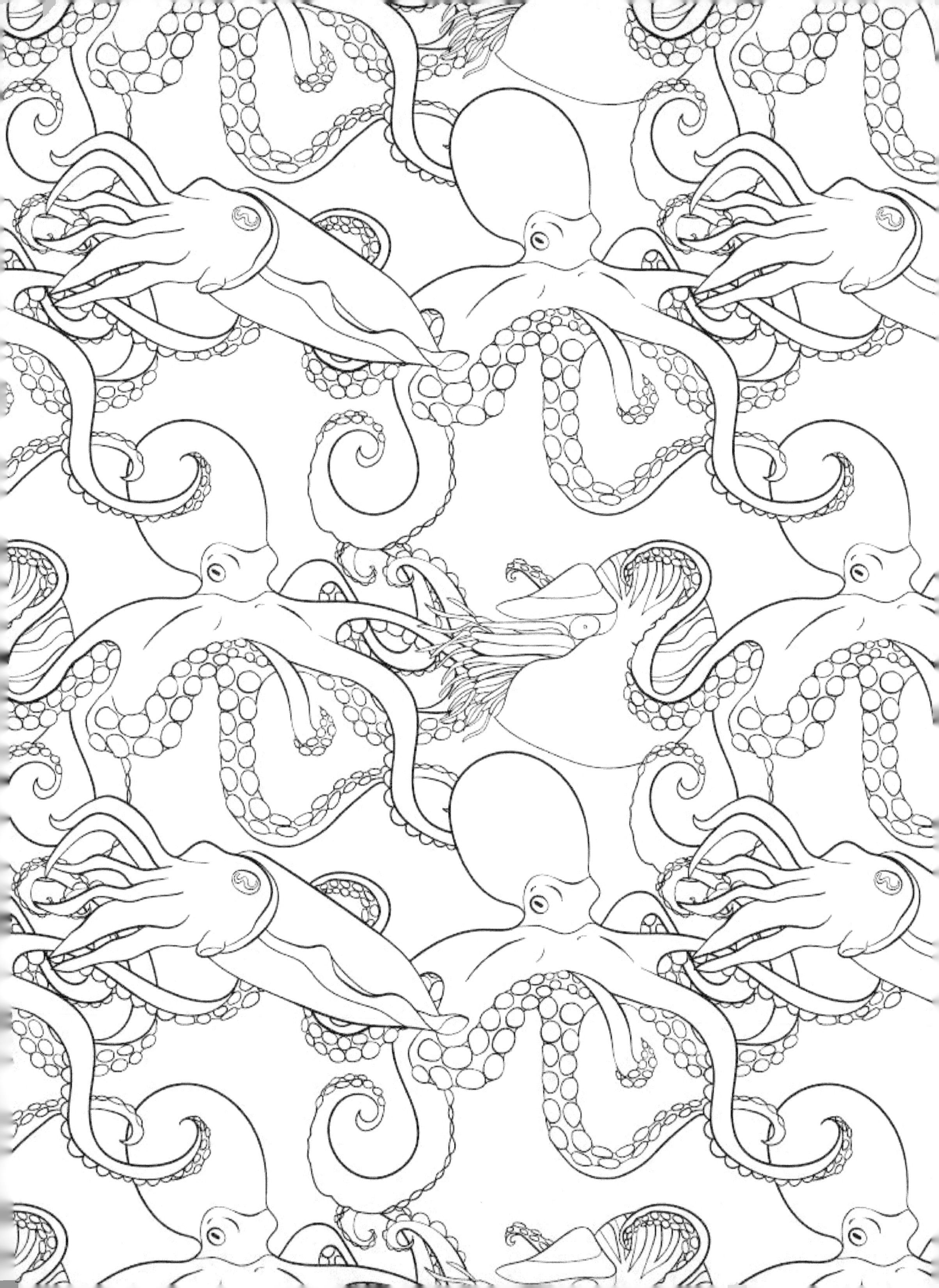

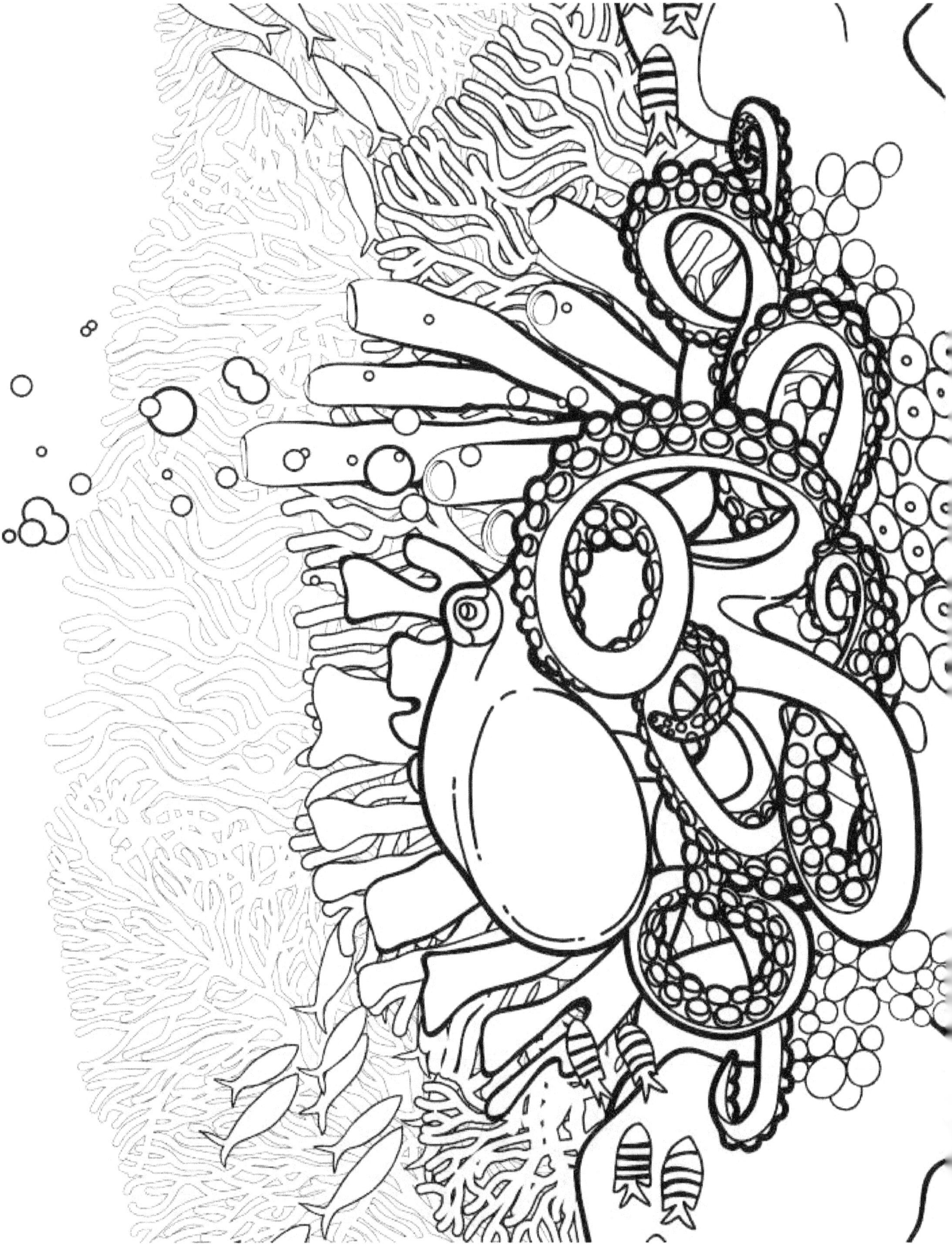

www.ingramcontent.com/pod-product-compliance
Lightning Source LLC
Chambersburg PA
CBHW081216170526
45165CB00009B/2840
* 9 7 8 1 5 4 7 2 4 8 3 3 9 *